Designs by
Emma
I0776851

ISBN-13: 978-1981579822
ISBN-10: 1981579826

i am emma criddle, and i am 7 years old. last year i got a dress design book for christmas and loved it! but it was only full of girl models, and the first 25 pages of the book were full of ideas and instructions.

i wanted to make a book with only a few instructions to get started. that way, i don't give you a whole lot of ideas. i want you to create clothes on your own! the other thing i wanted to change was to make a book for boys and girls... because some girls like to draw boy clothes, and some boys like to draw girl clothes!

i wanted my book to be the world's first design book for kids, by a kid, for all of those future clothing designers. when i grow up, i want to make dresses, and i spend a lot of my time making and designing dresses now! so this is my gift to you.

if you want one of your best designs to become a real article of clothing, or even a whole design company, you can email me at emma@emmacriddle.com - and my daddy's companies will help make your clothes a reality - just like mine!

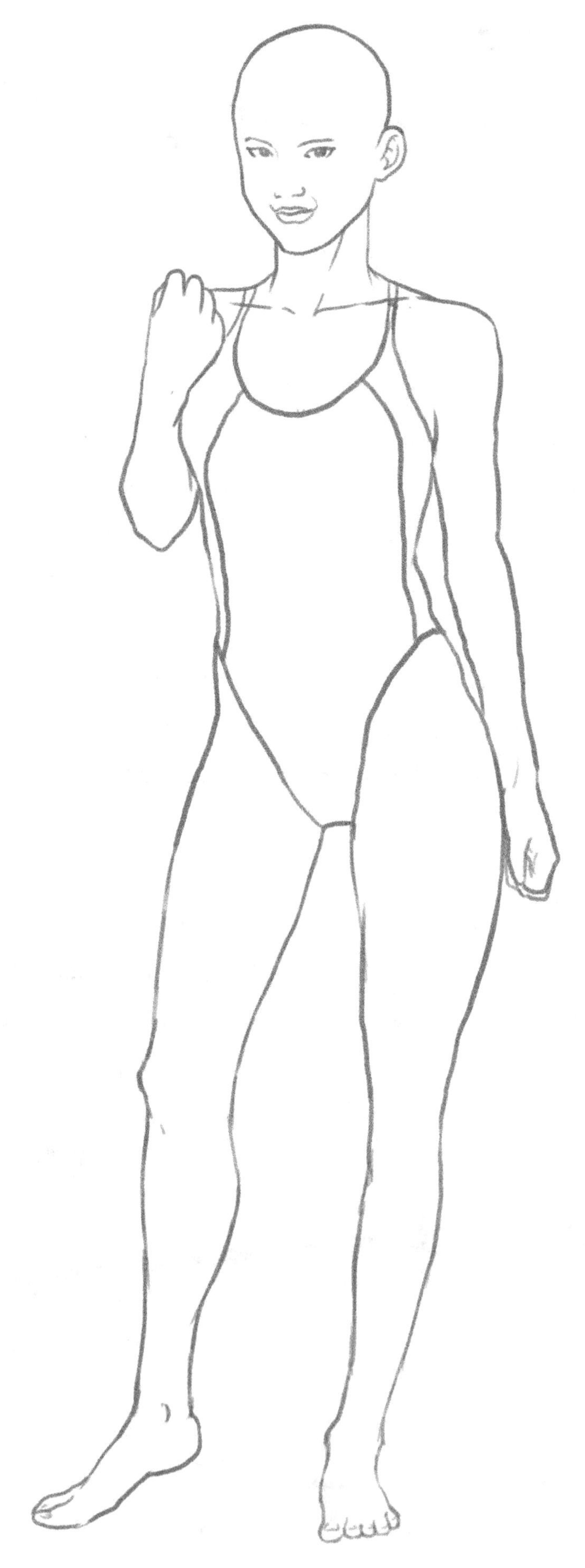

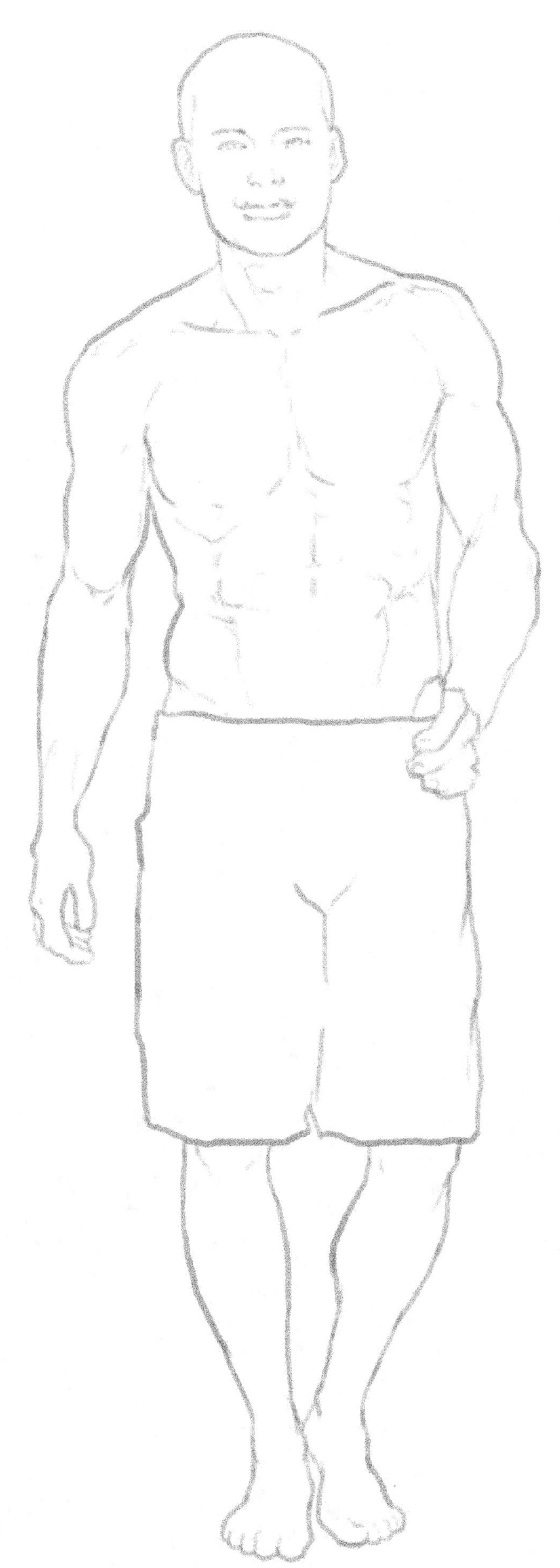

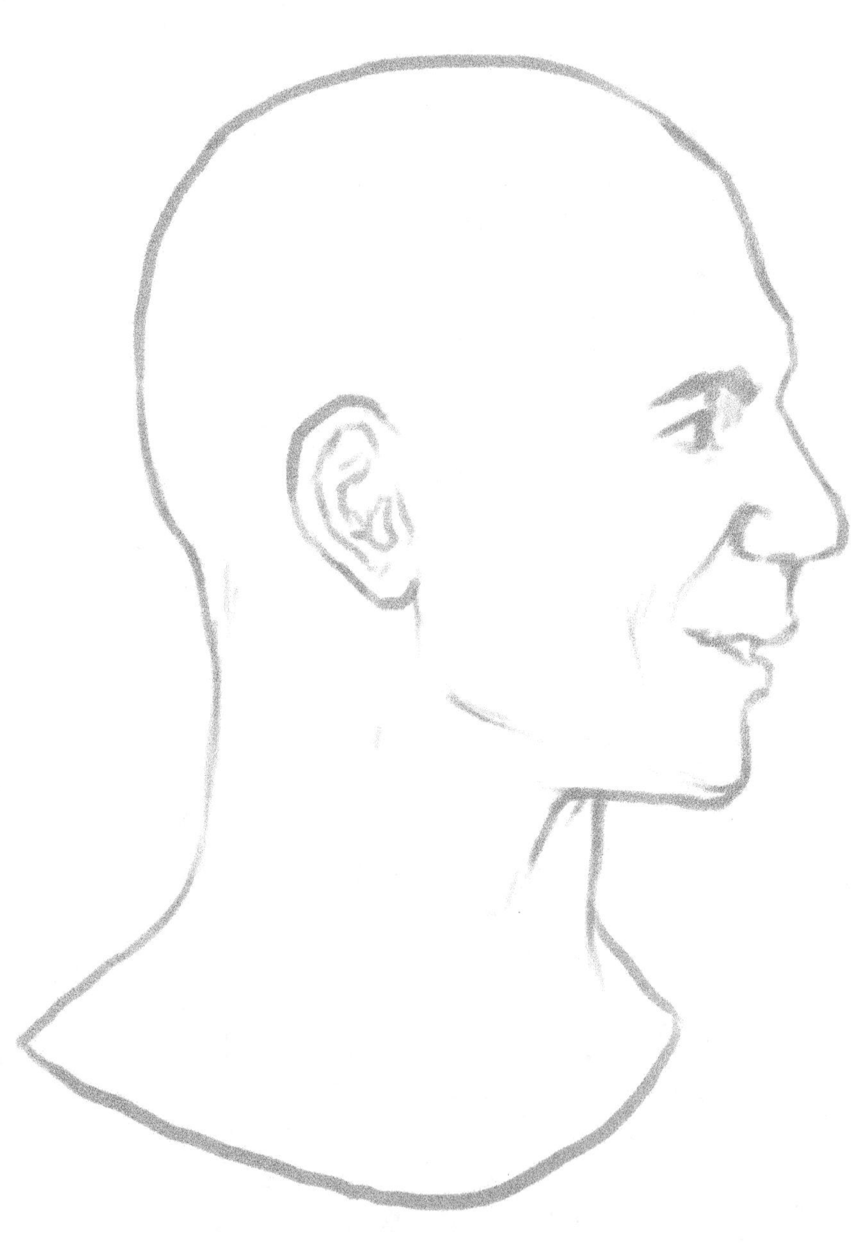

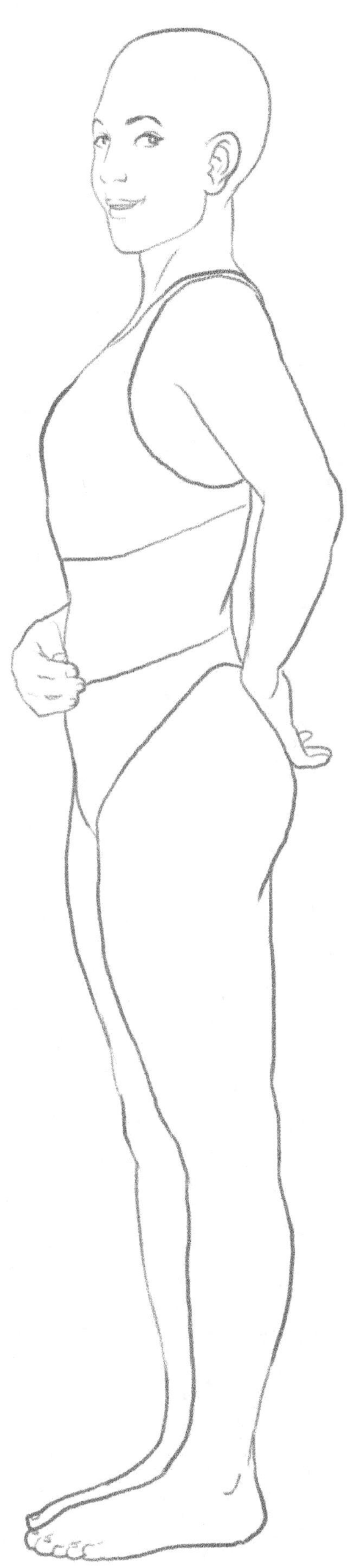

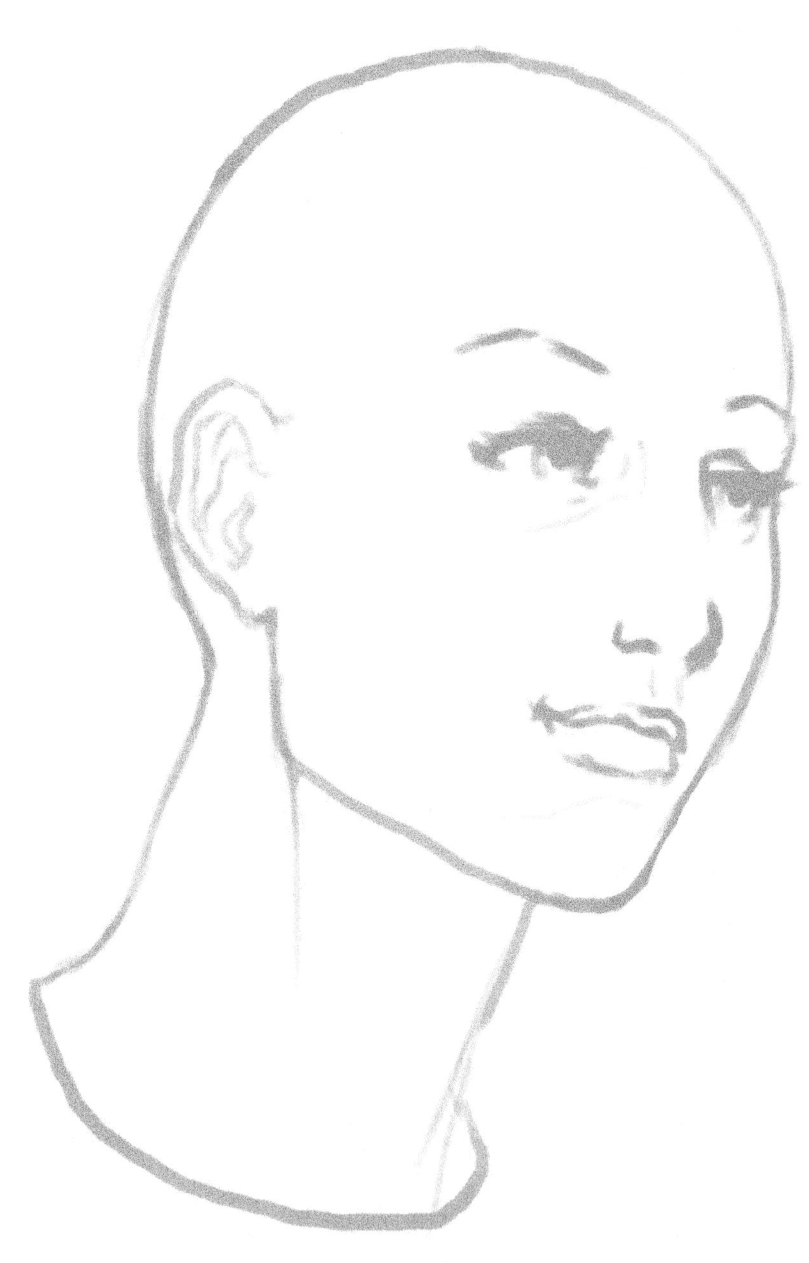

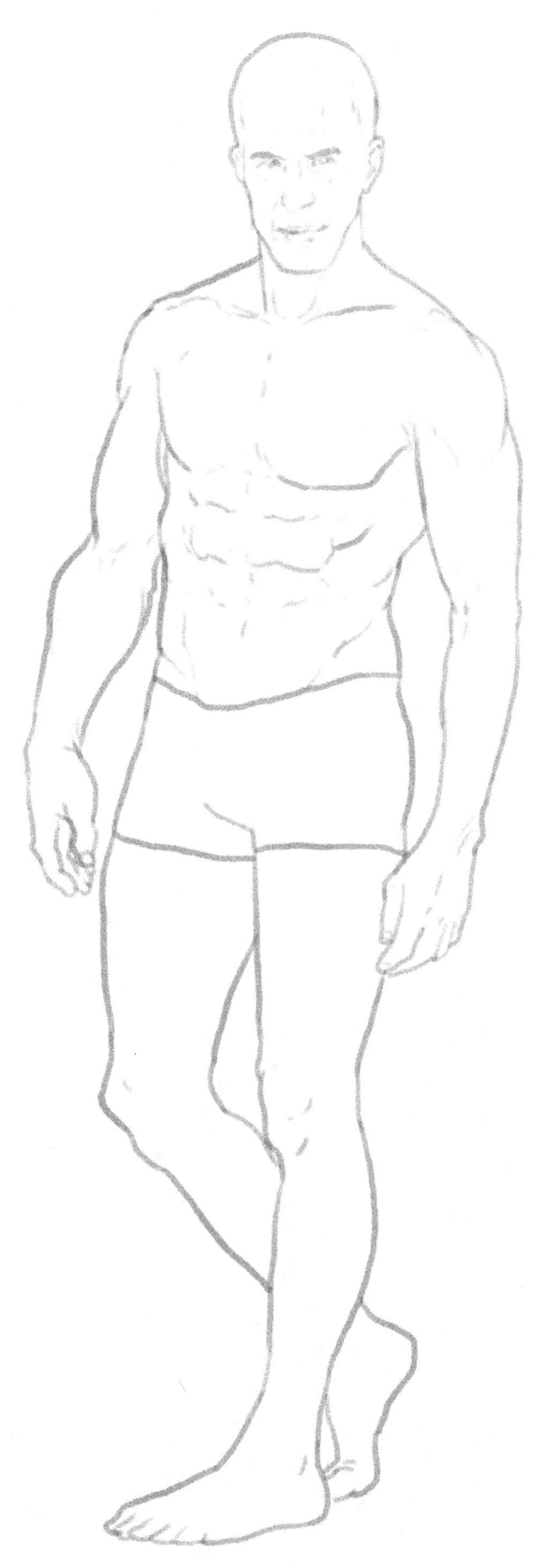

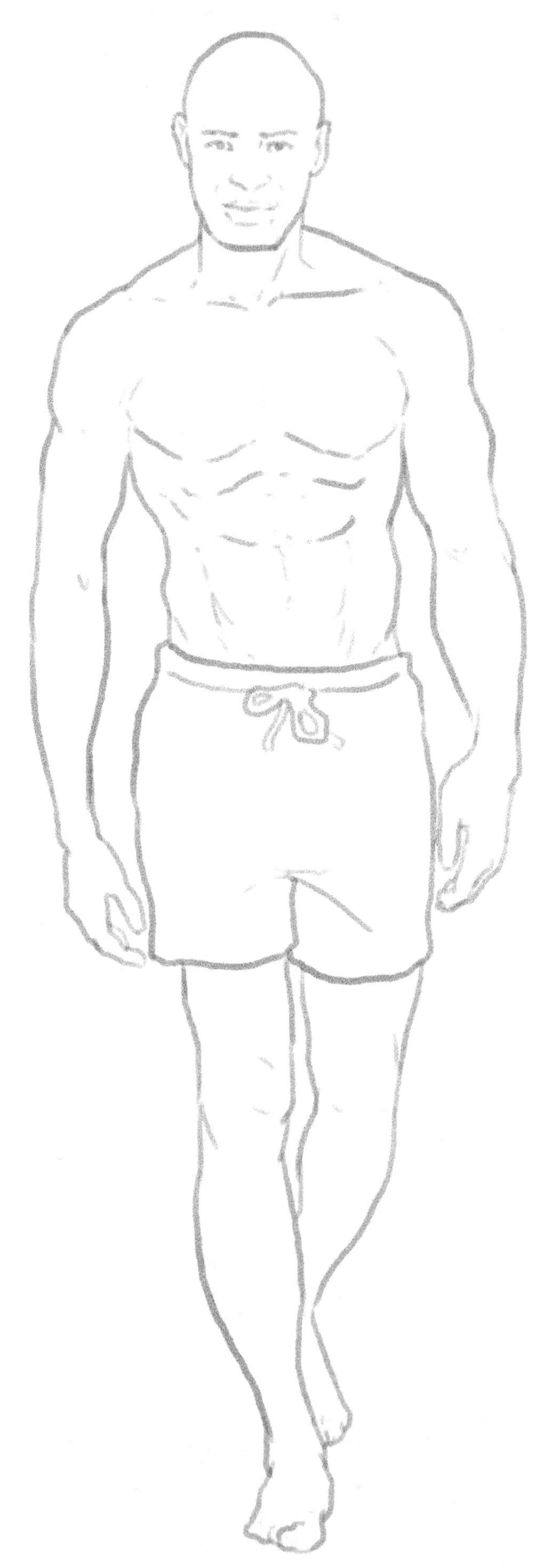

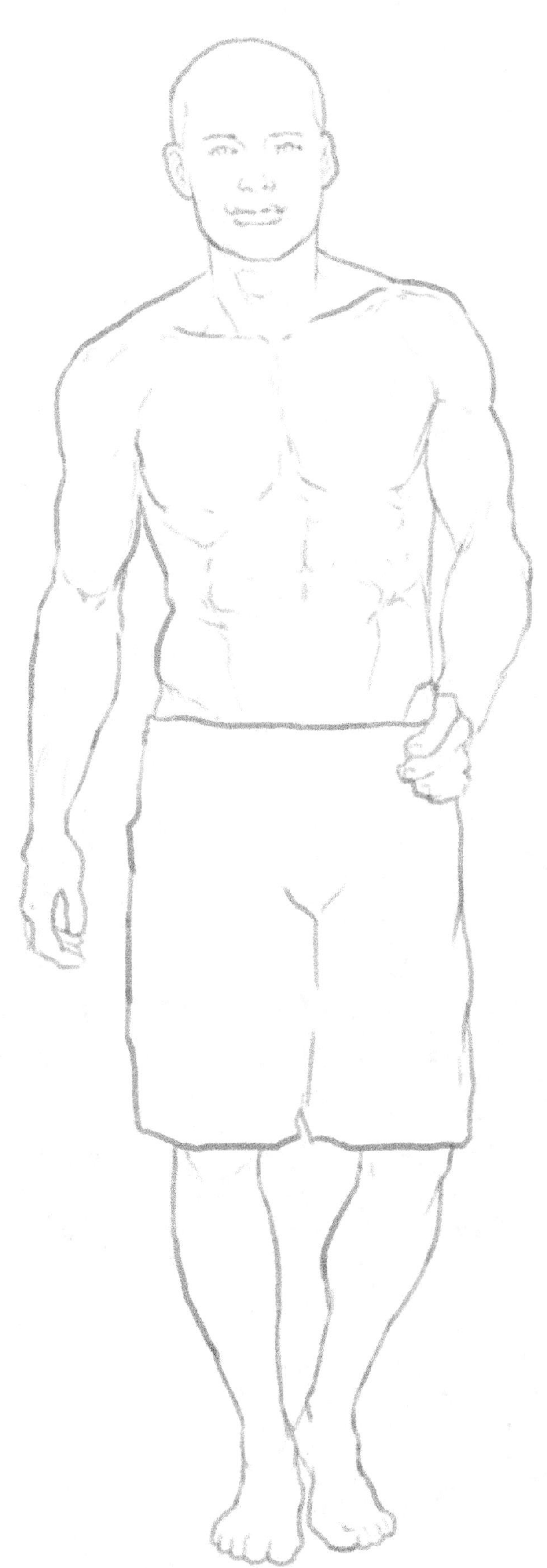

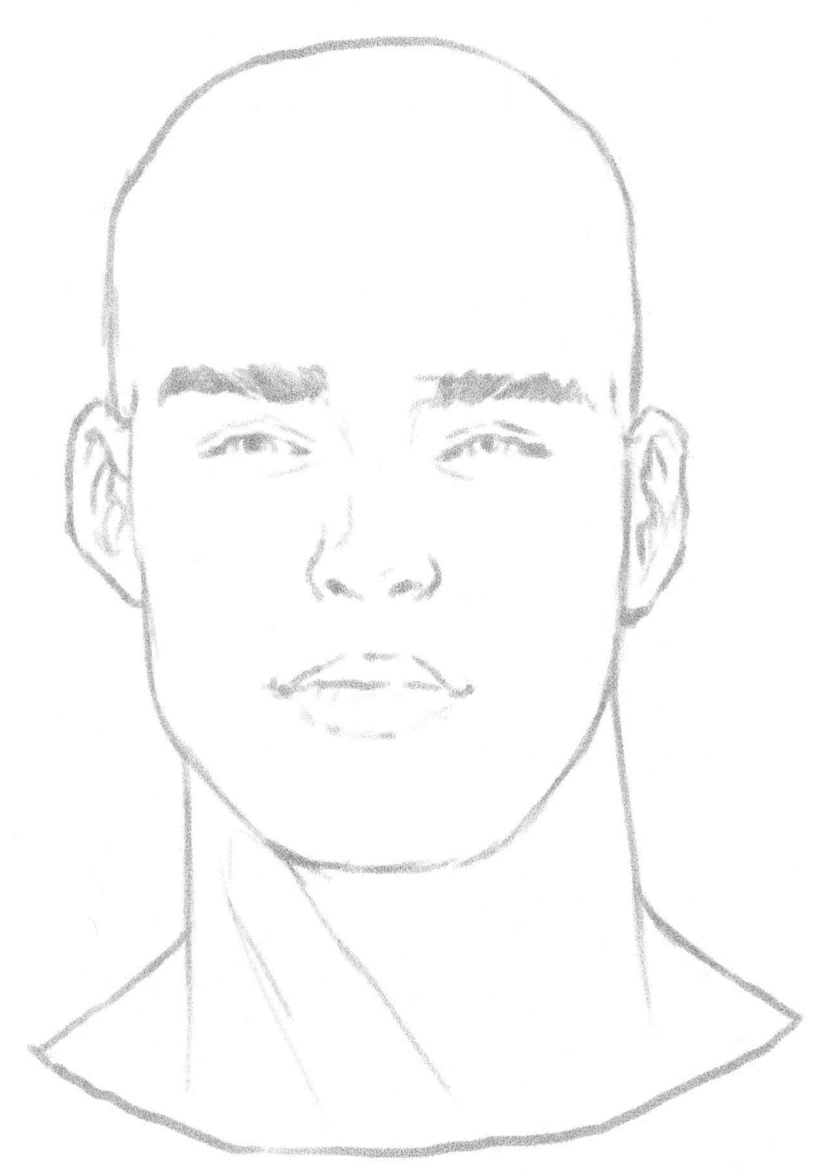

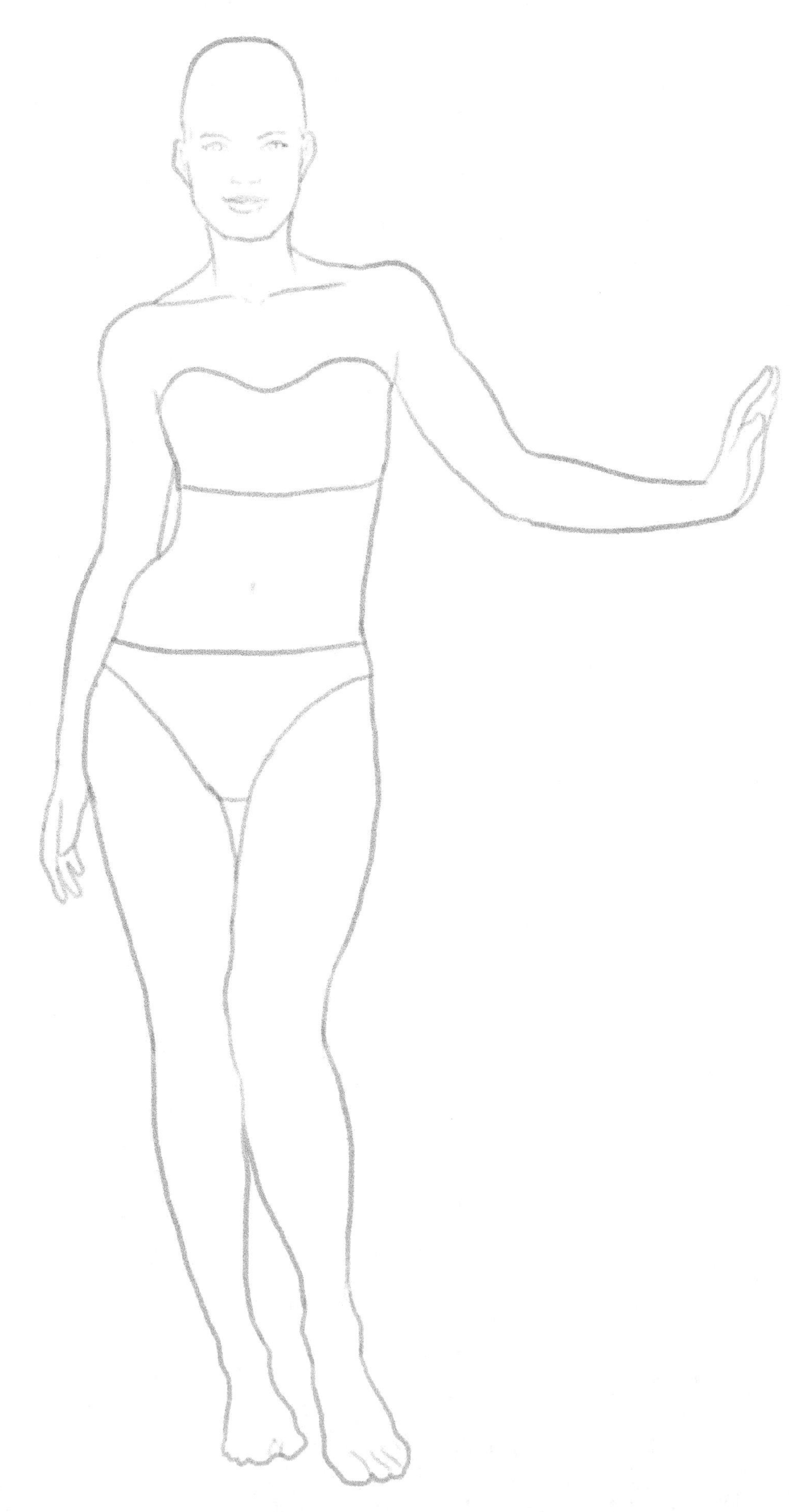

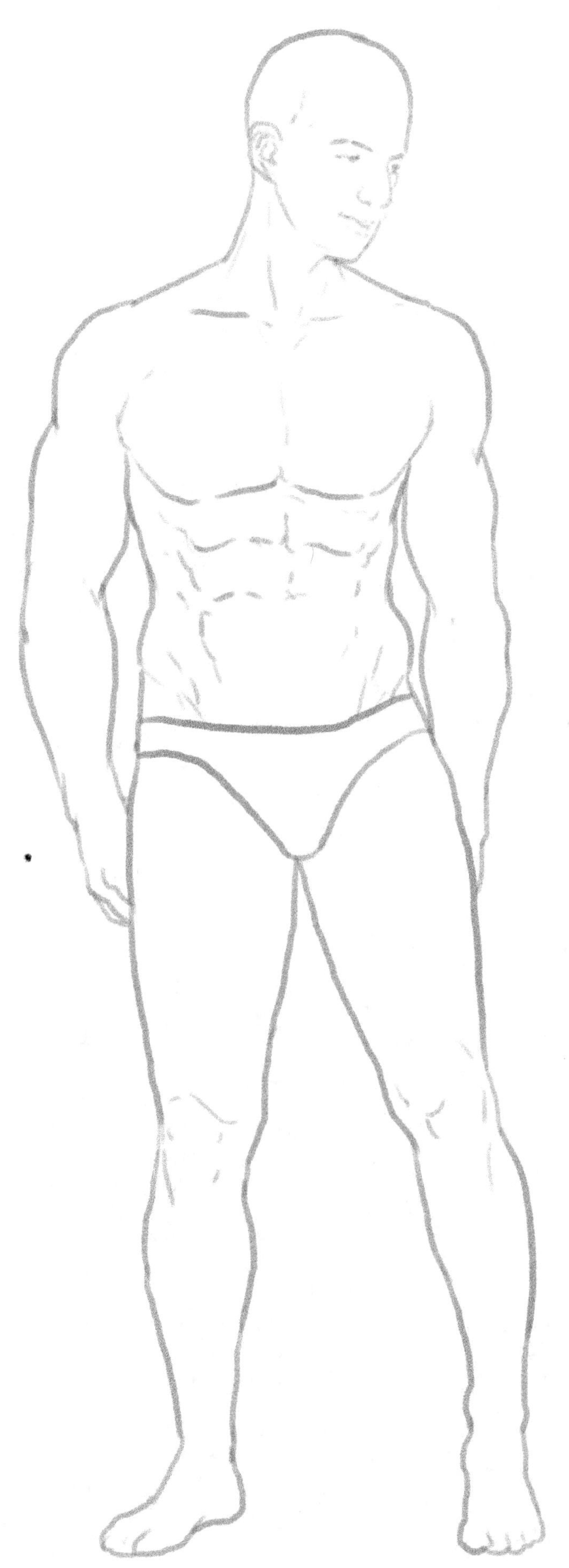

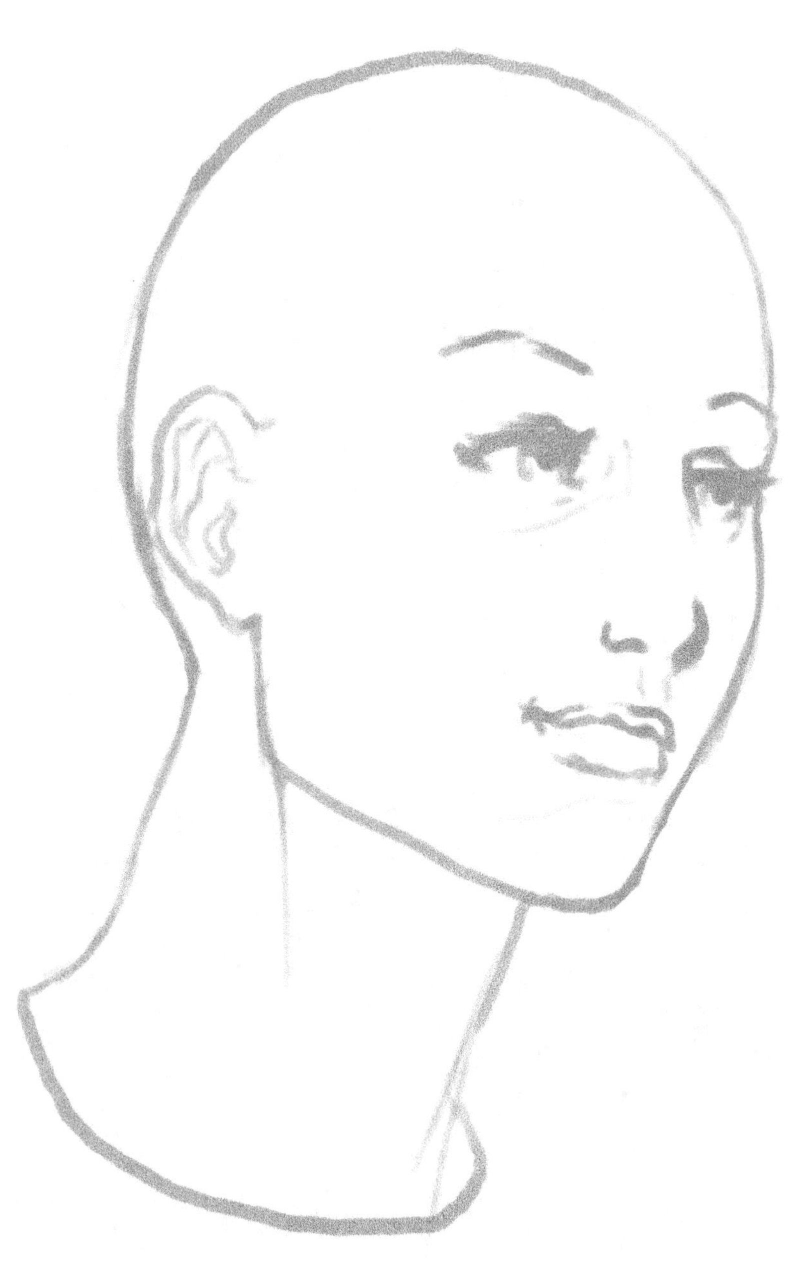

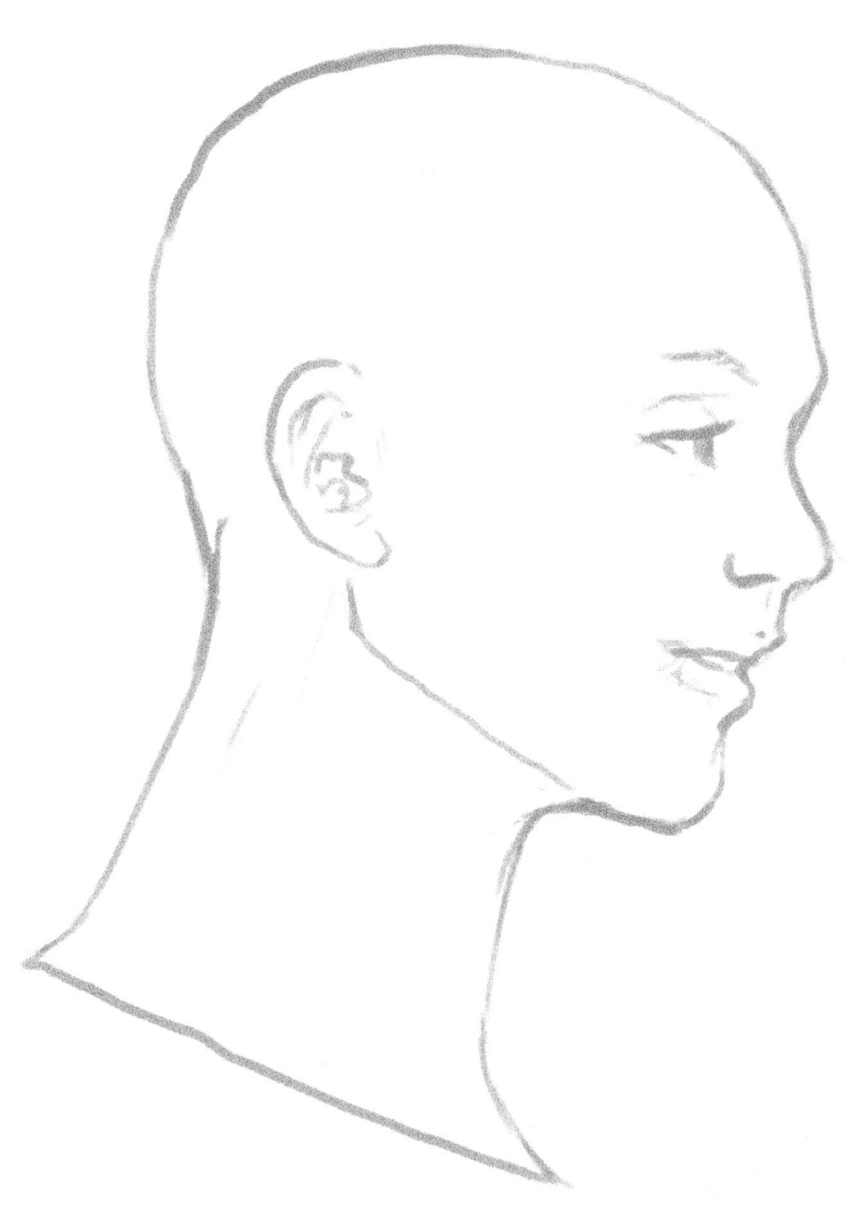

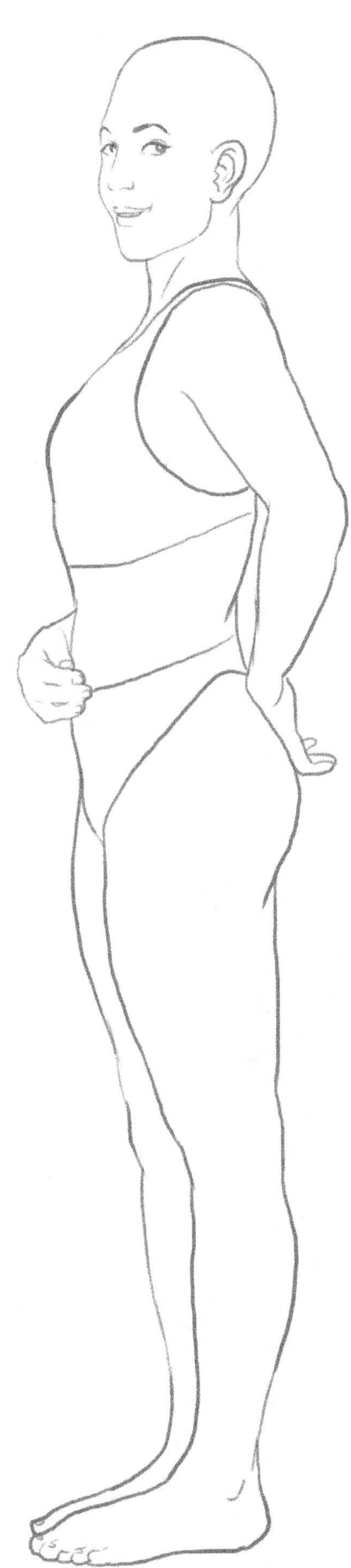

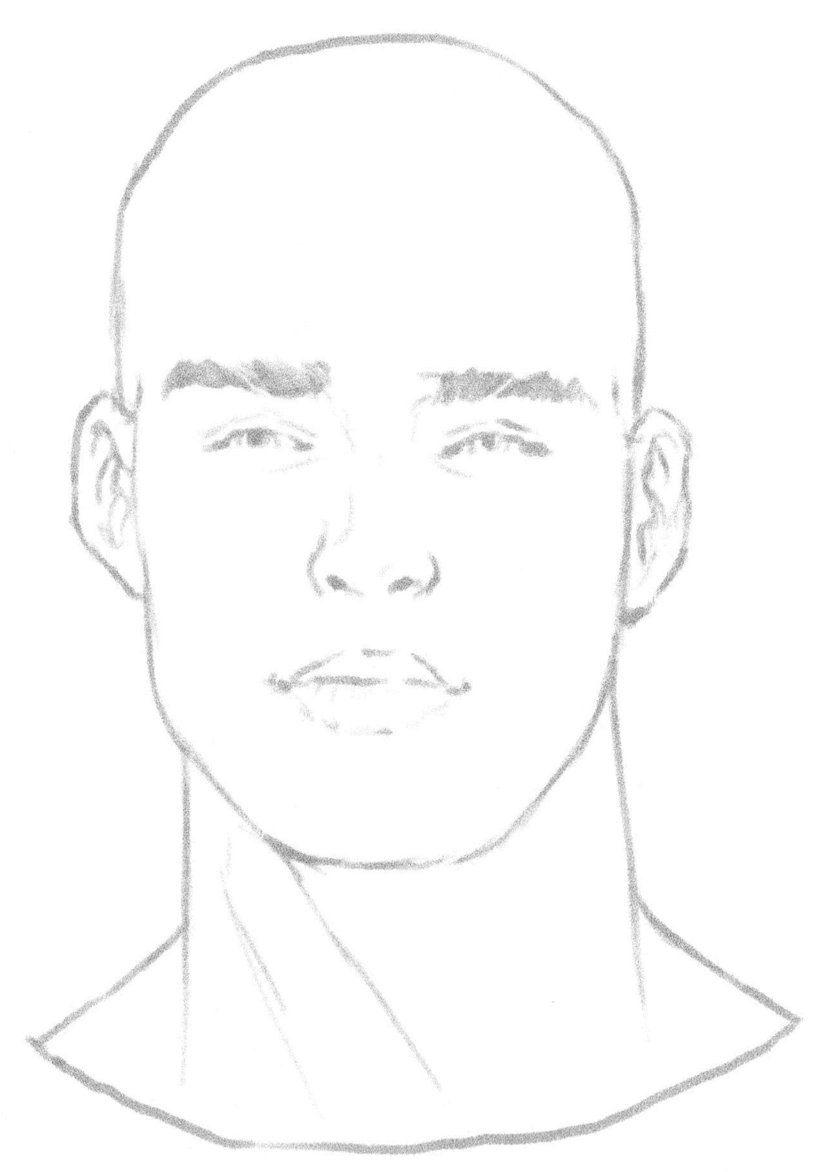

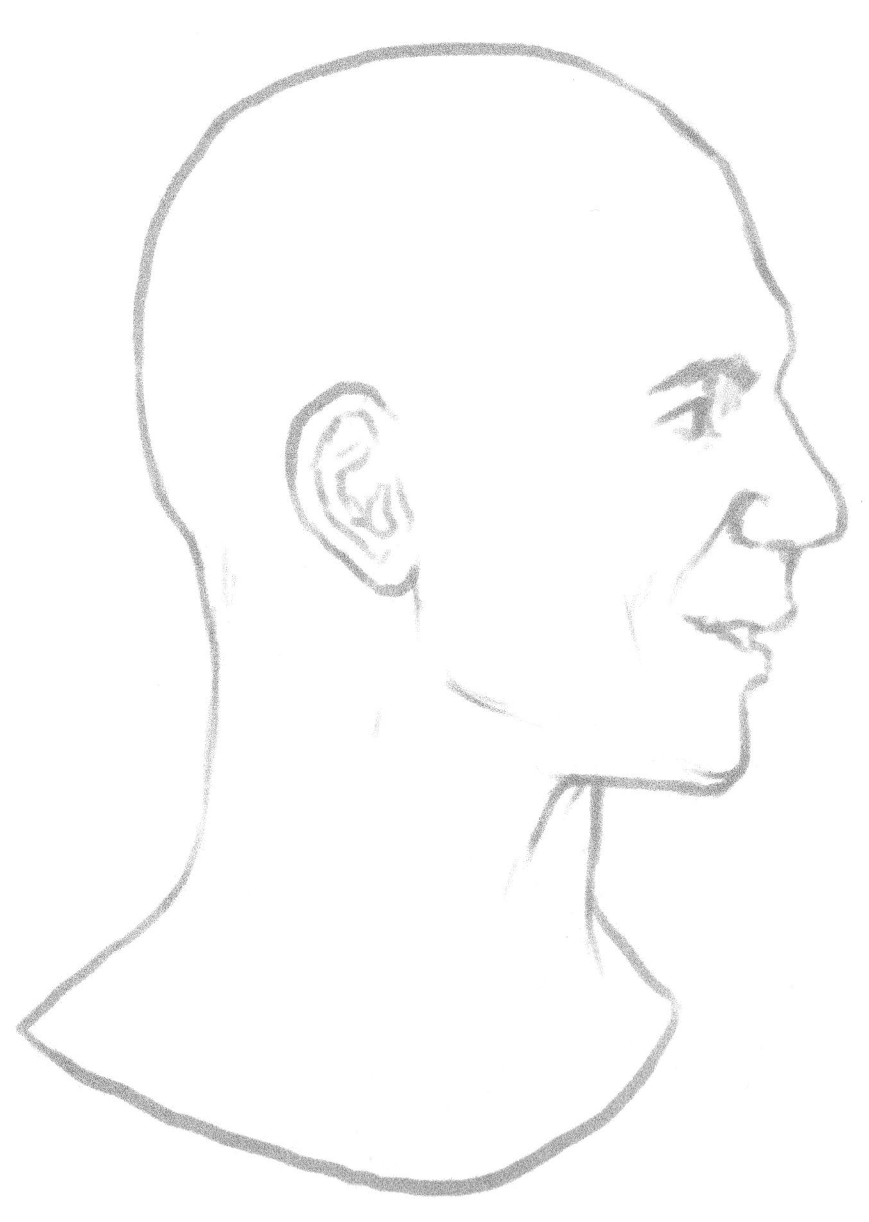

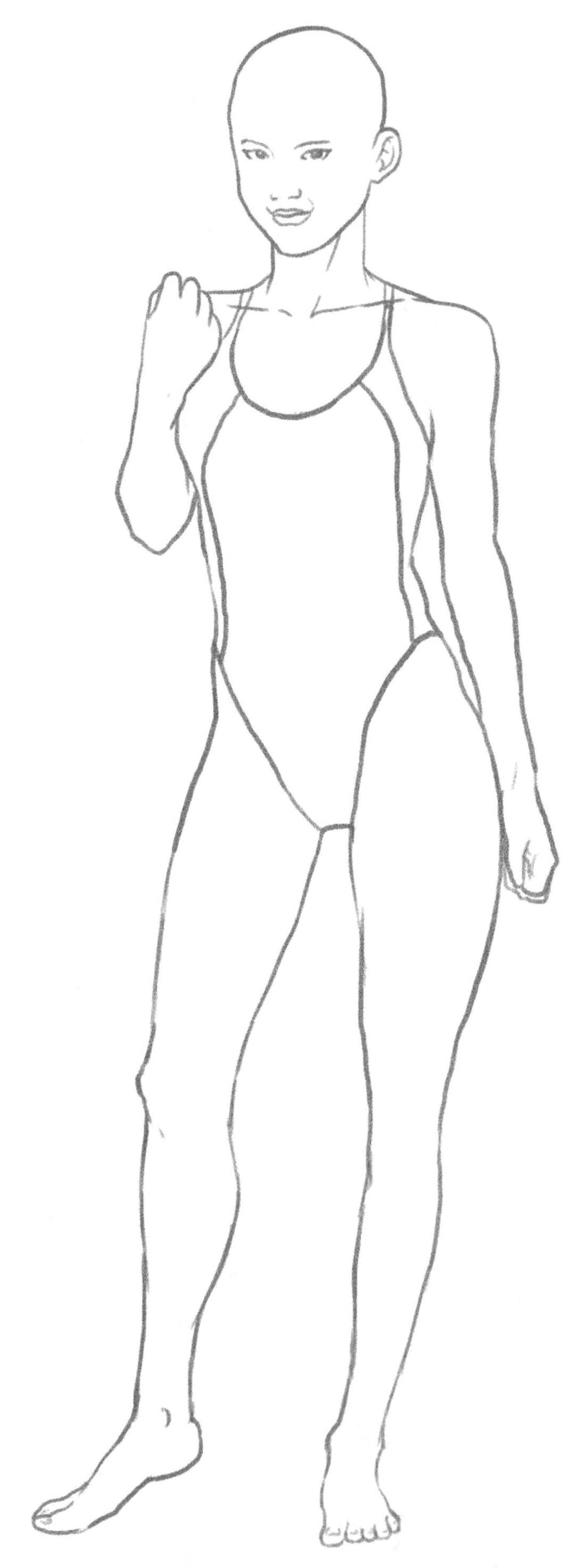

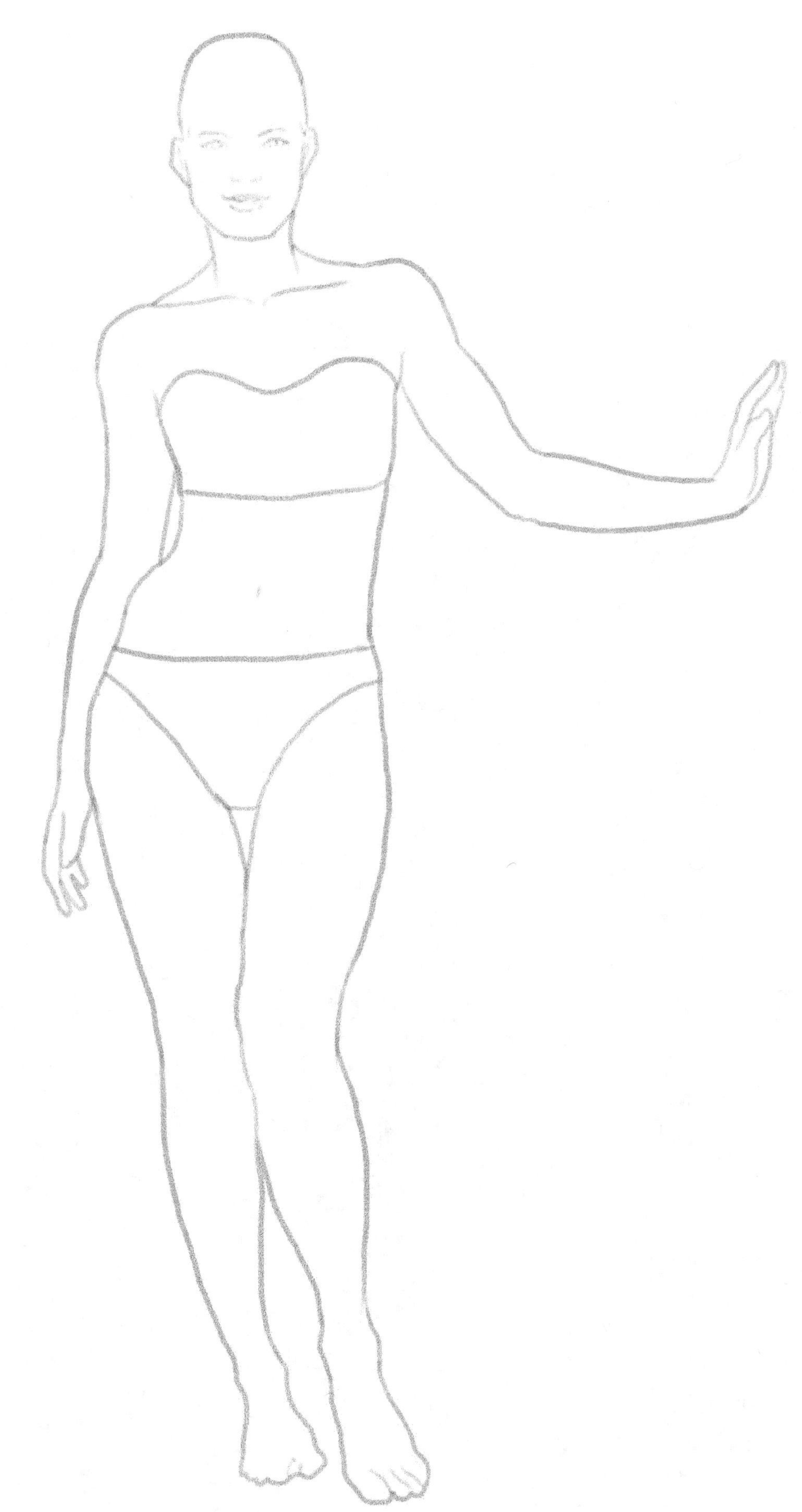

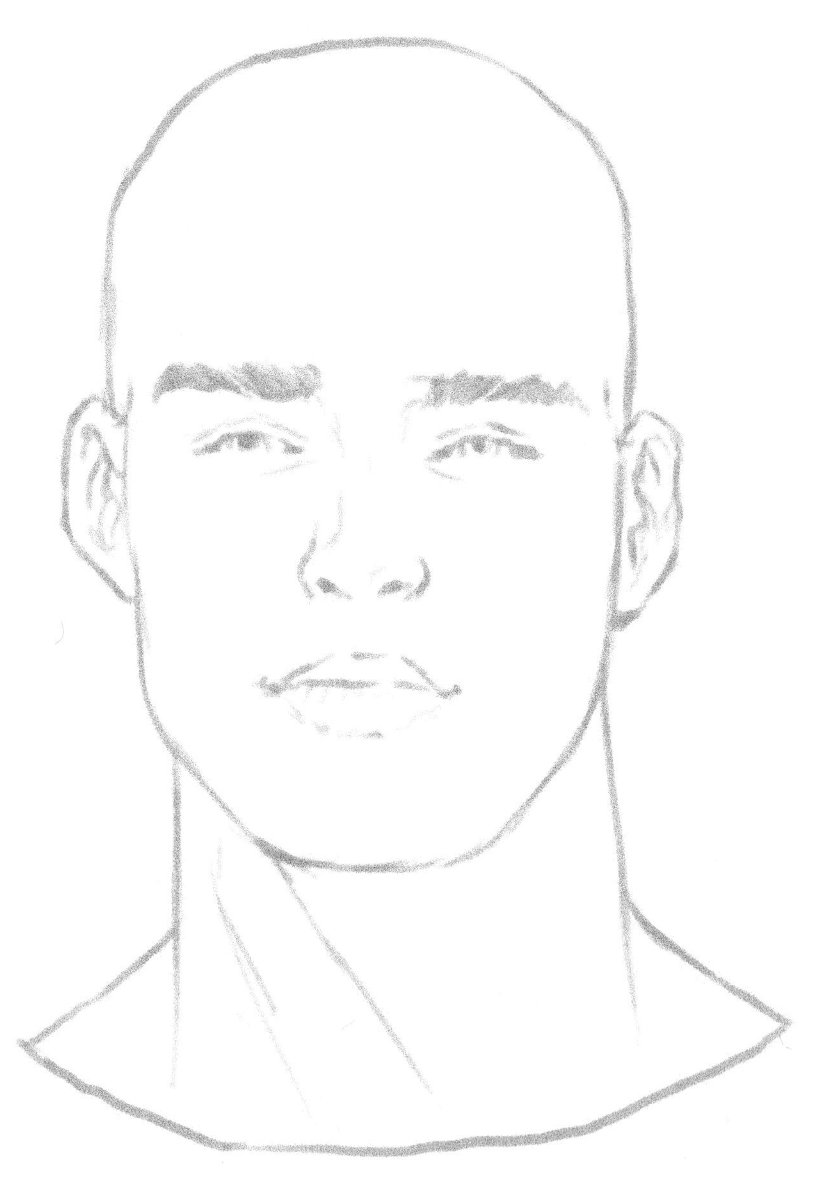

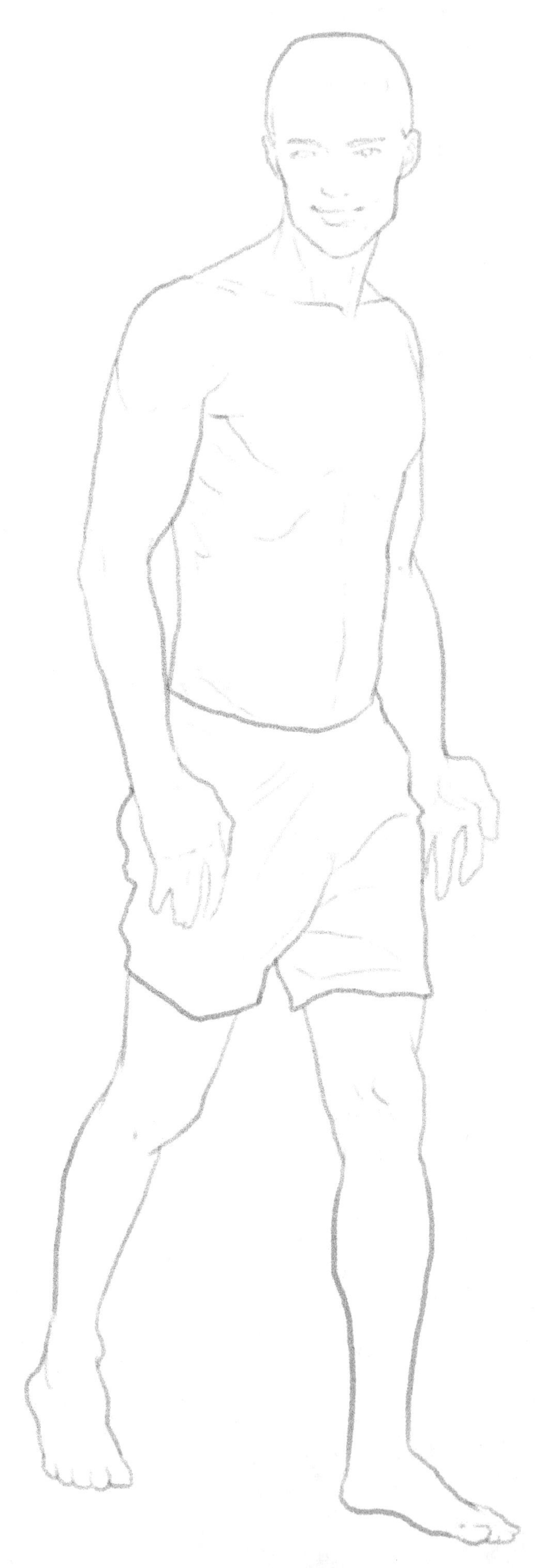

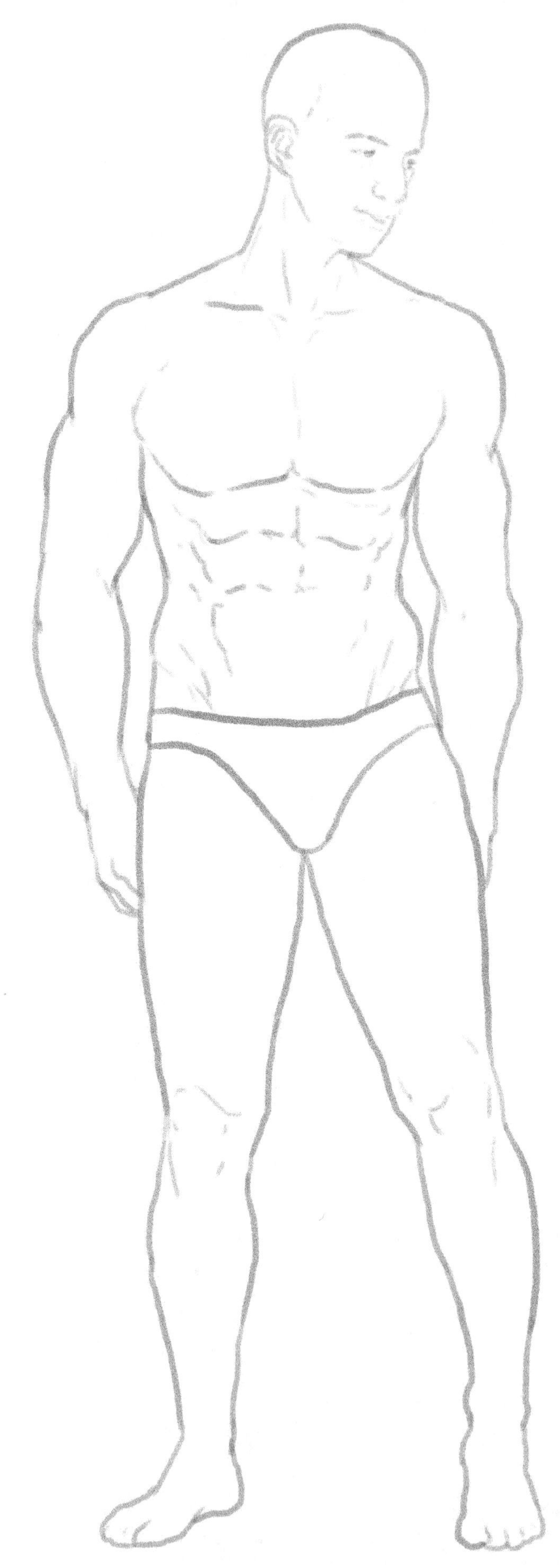

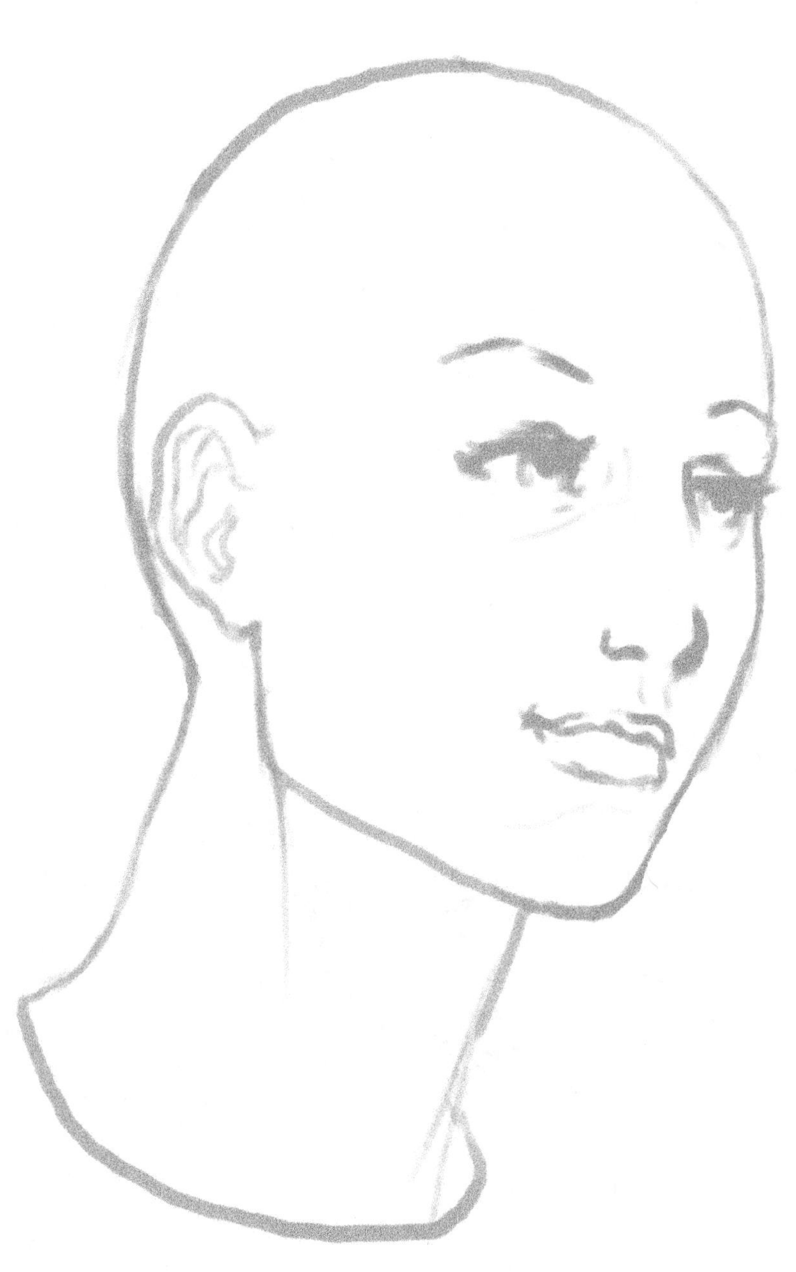

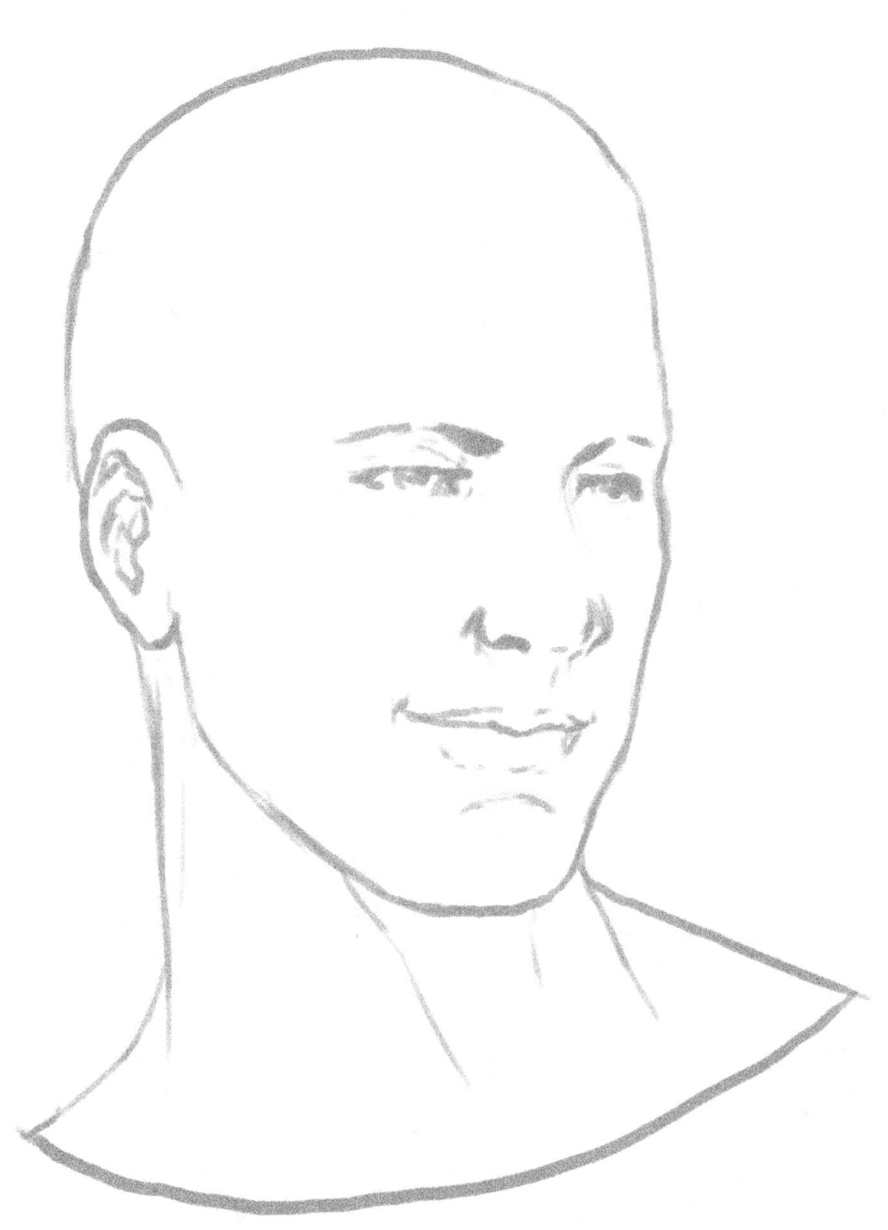

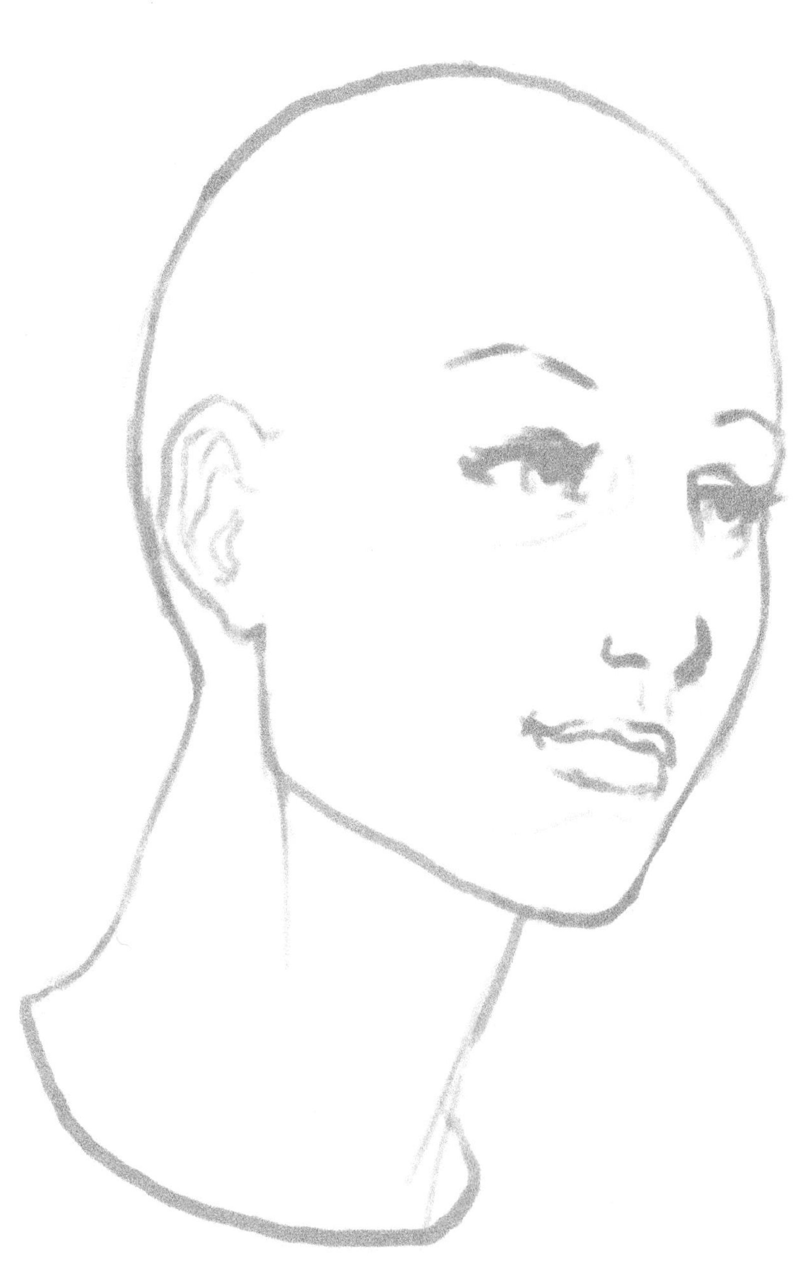

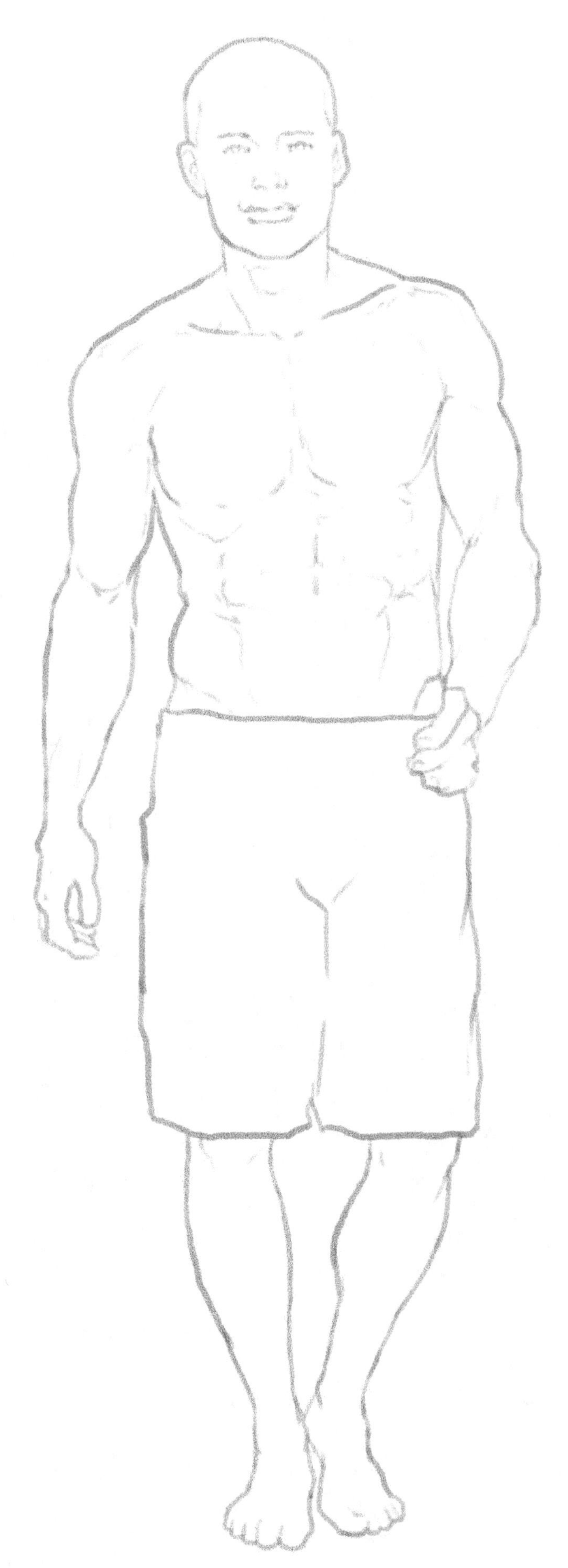

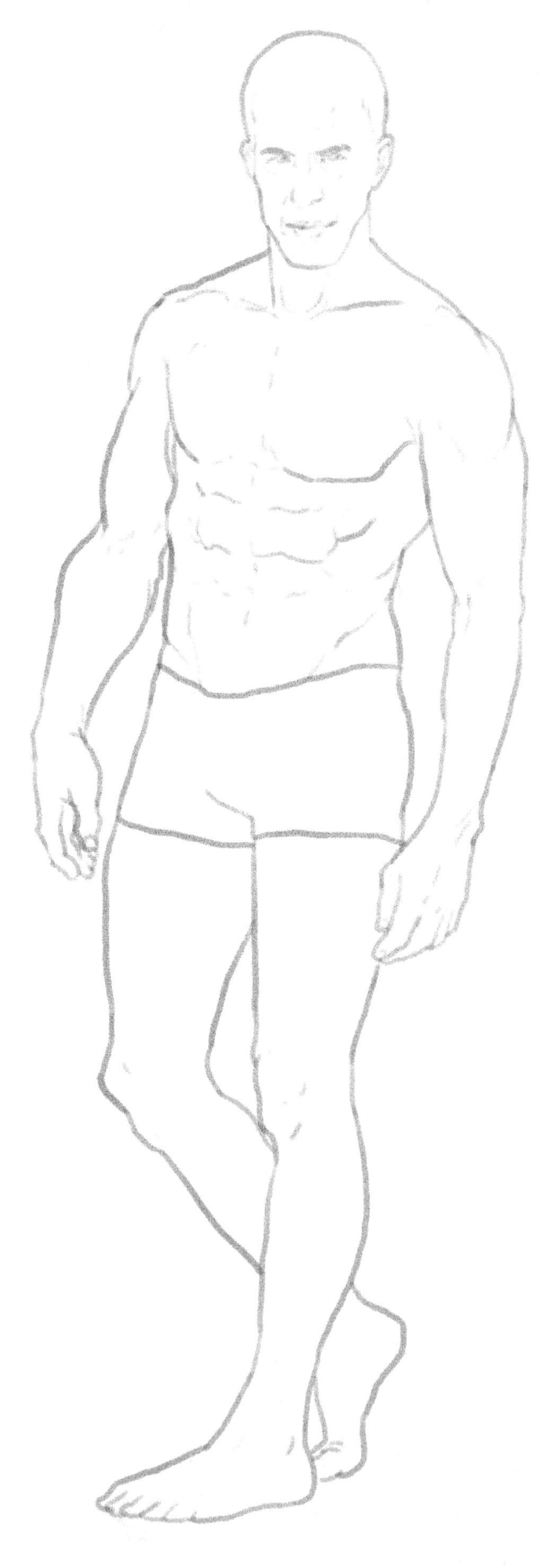

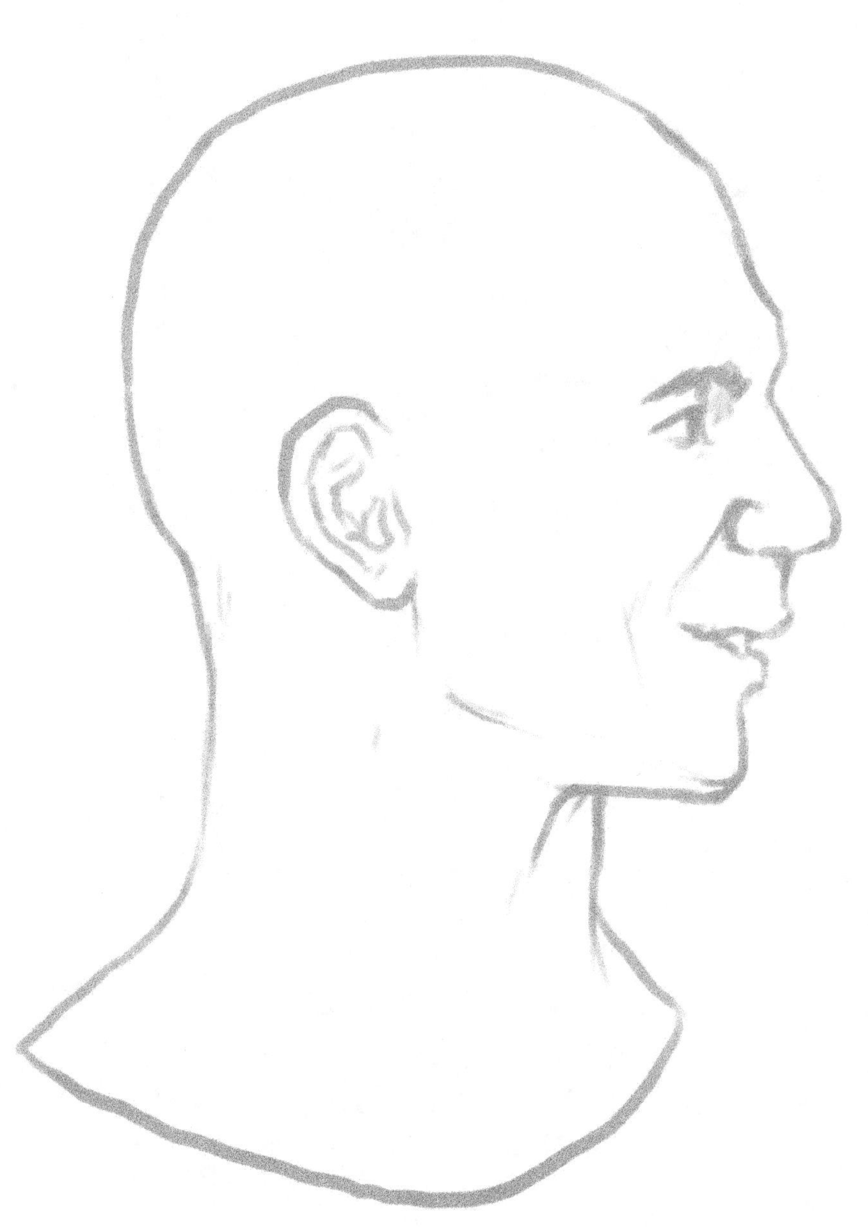

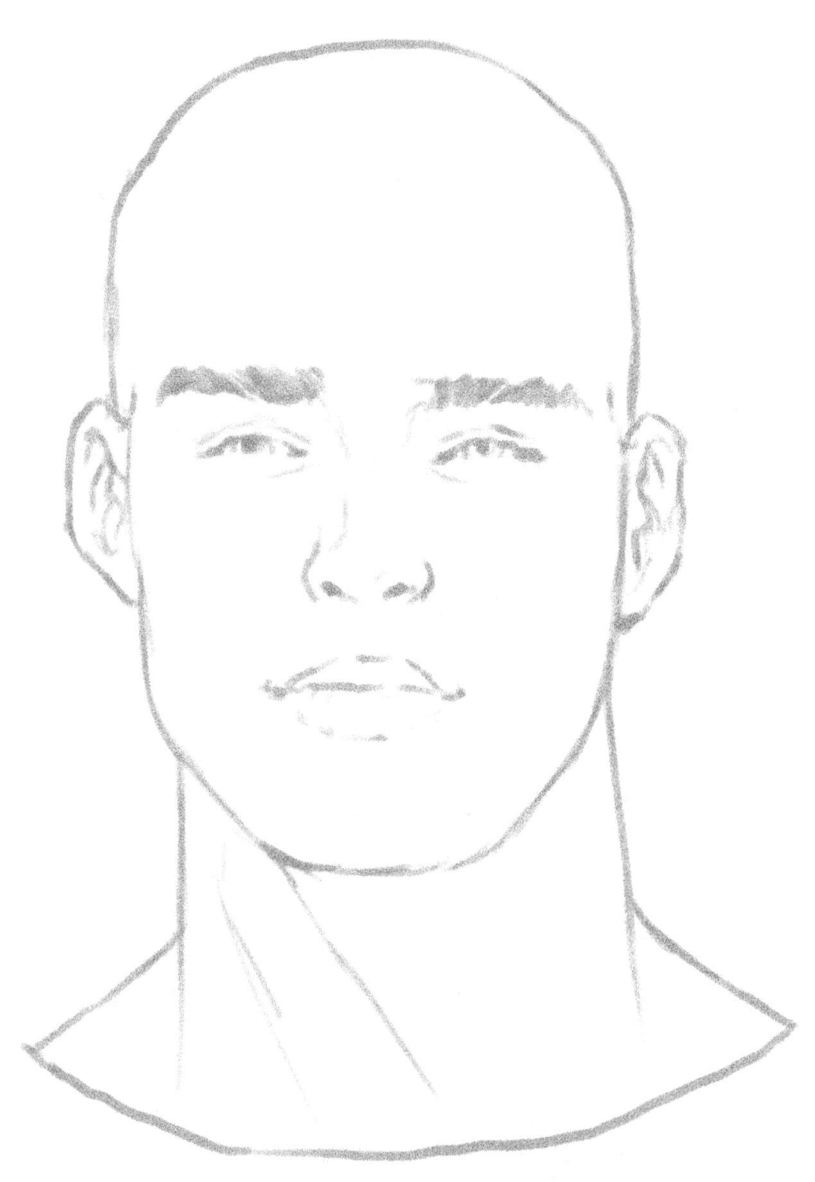

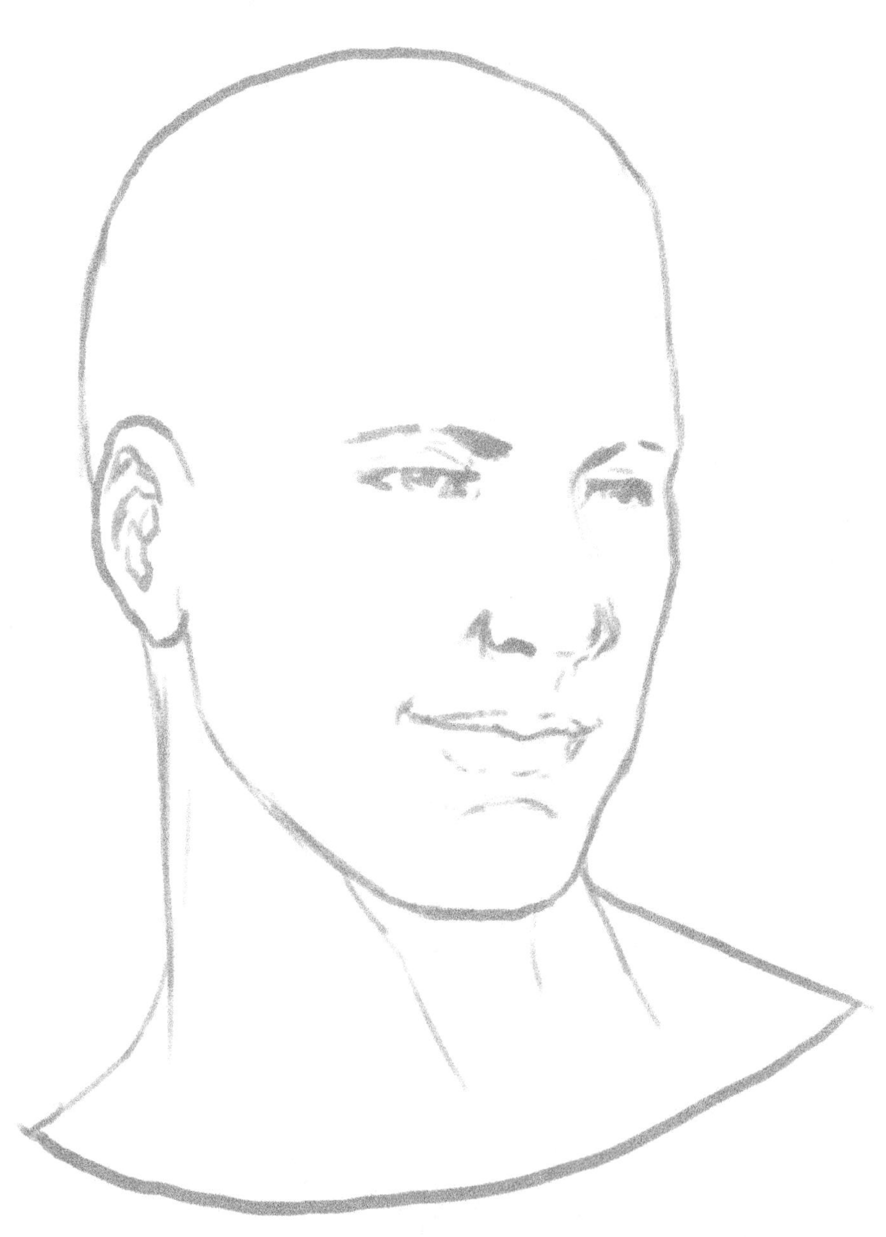

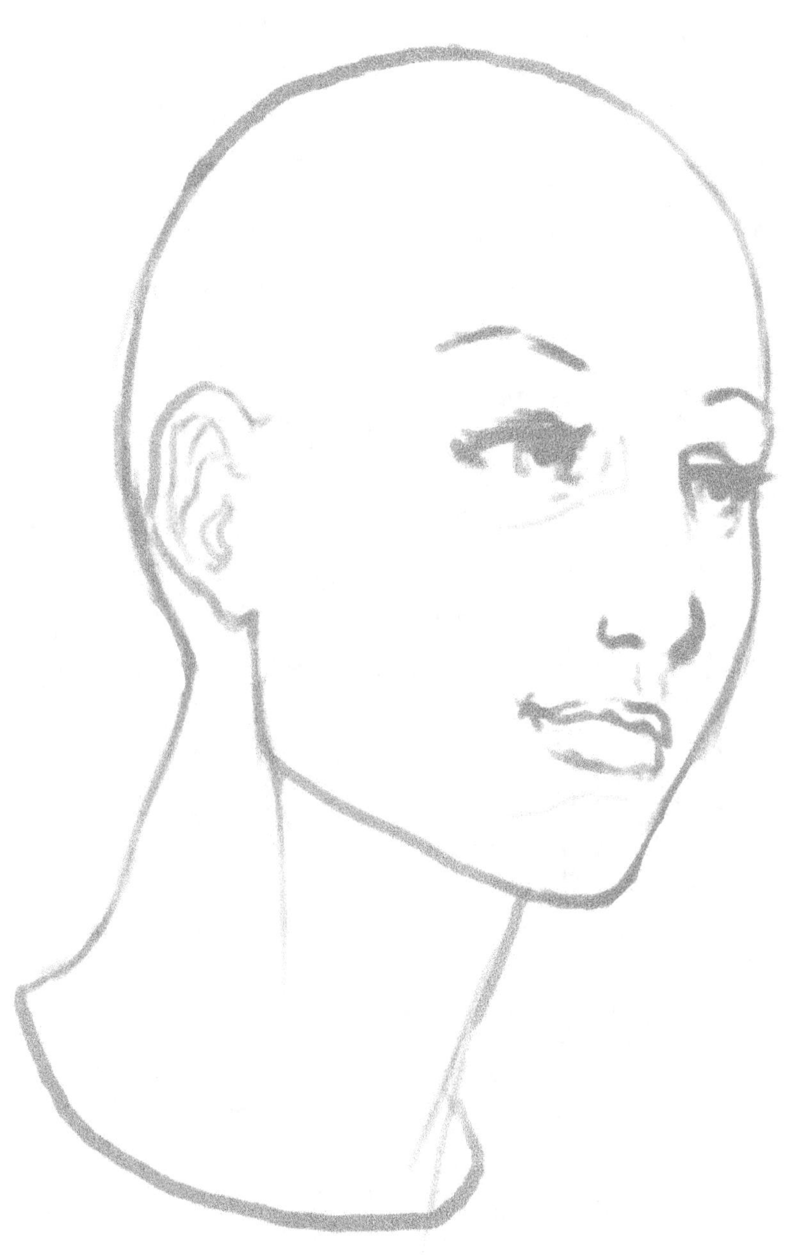

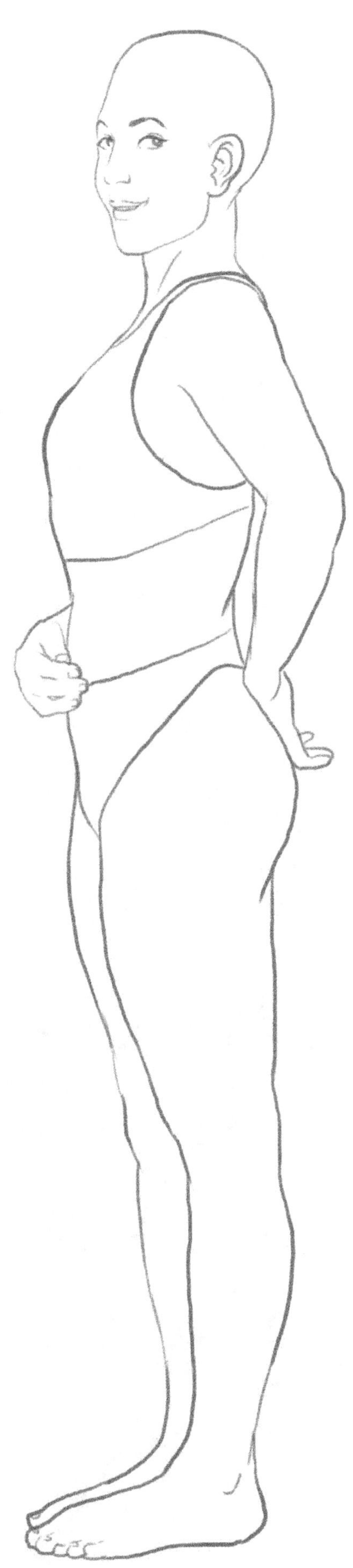

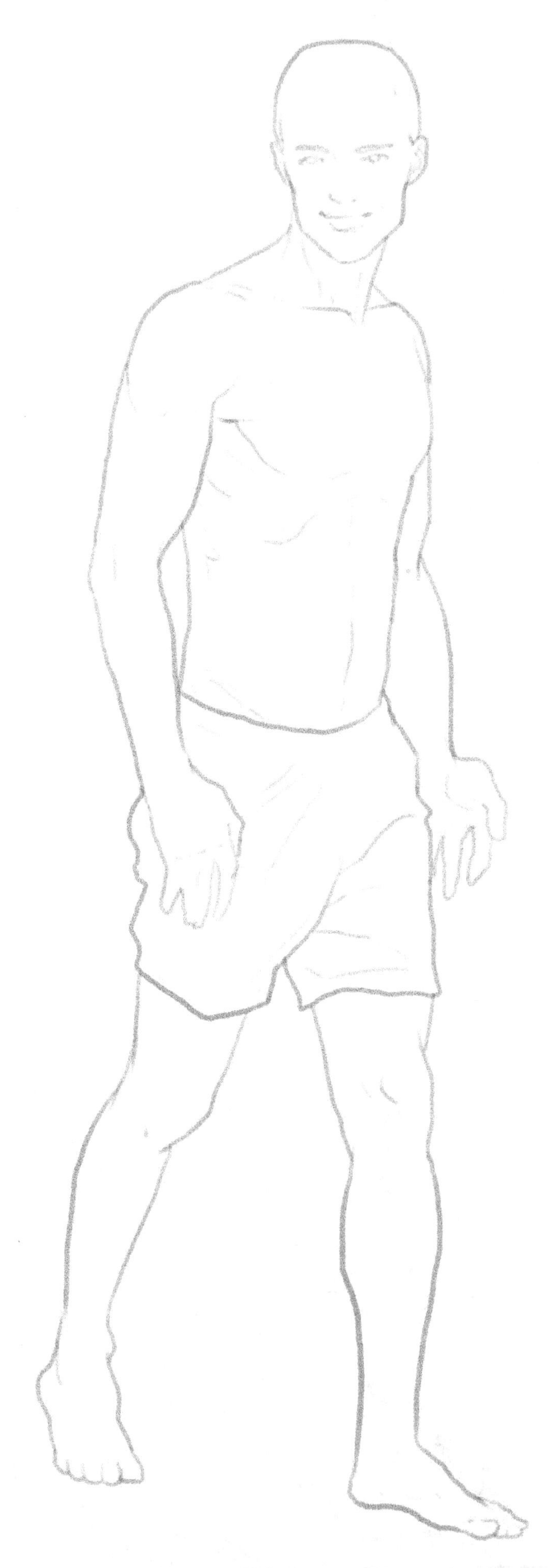

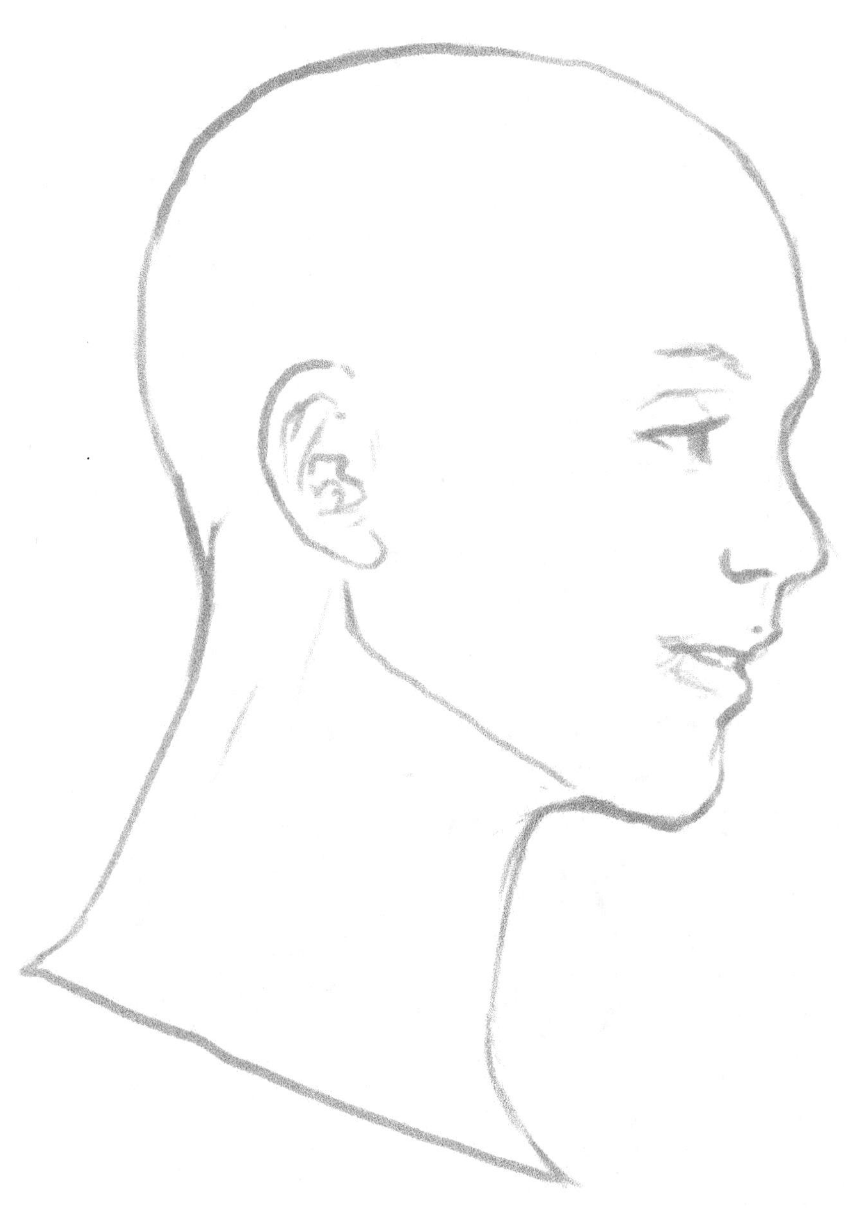

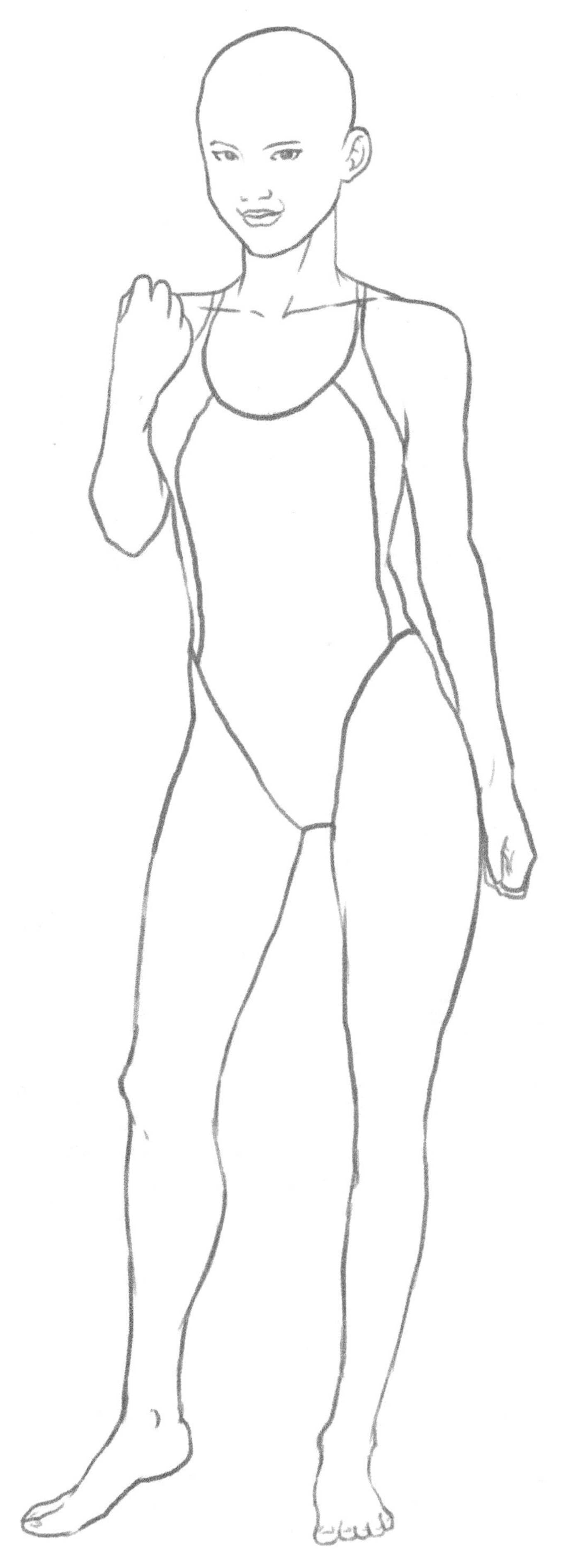

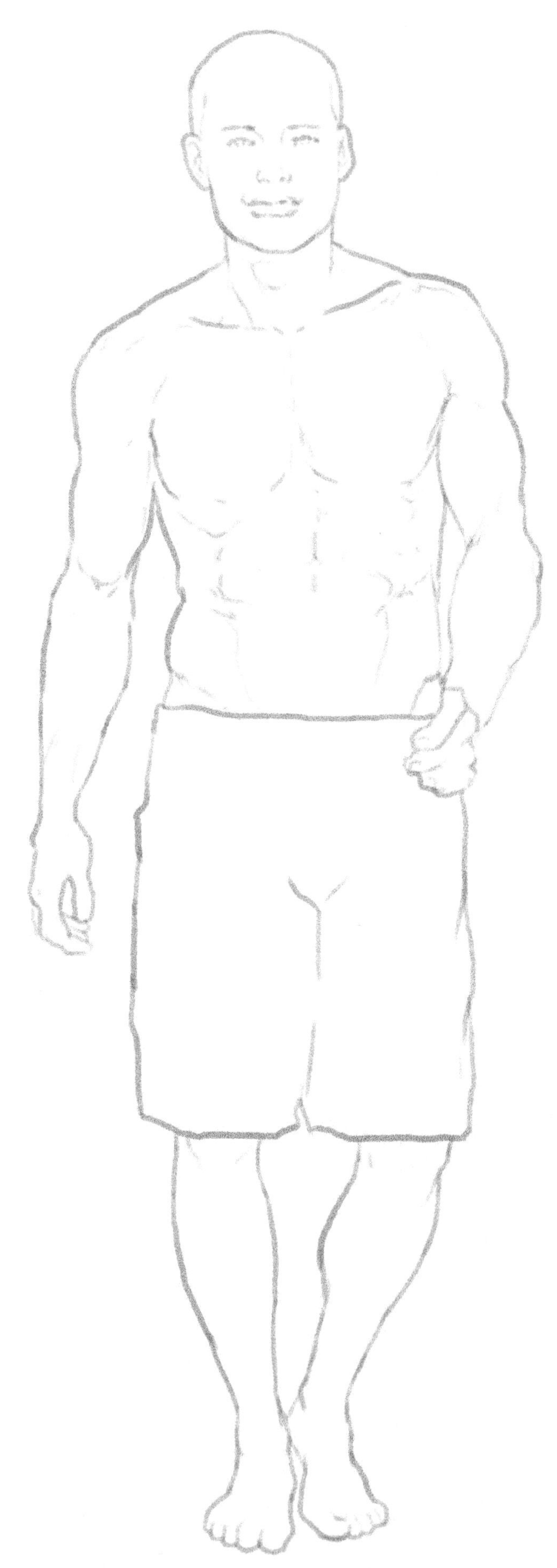

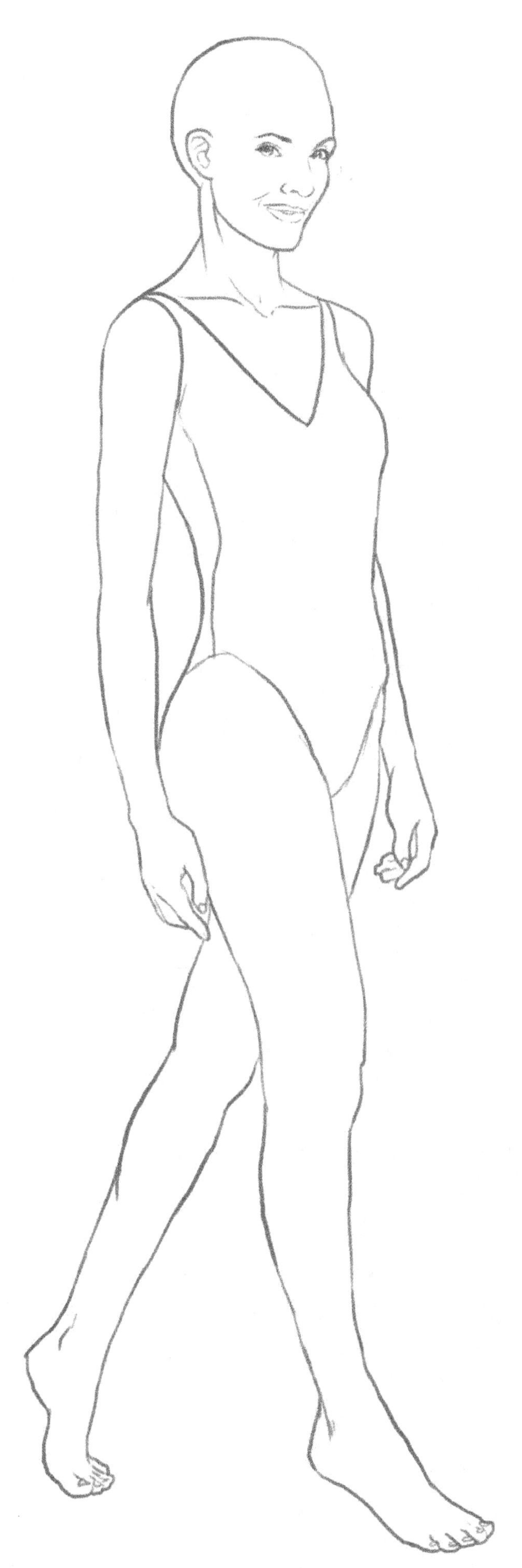

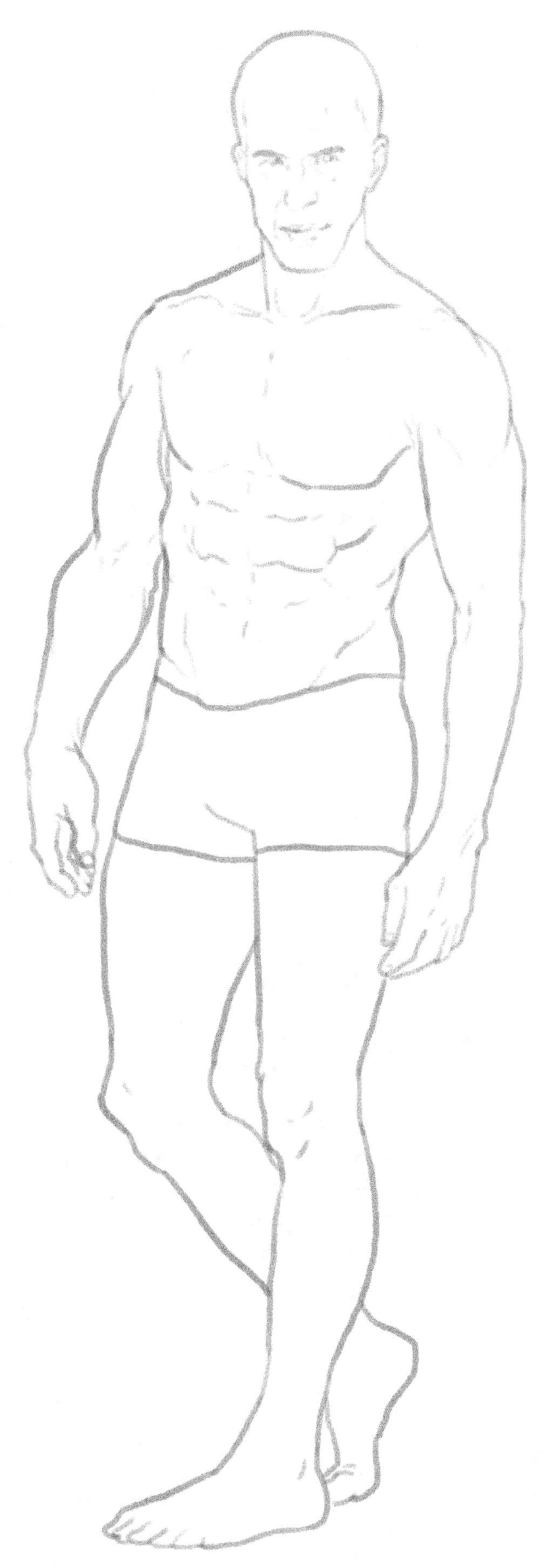

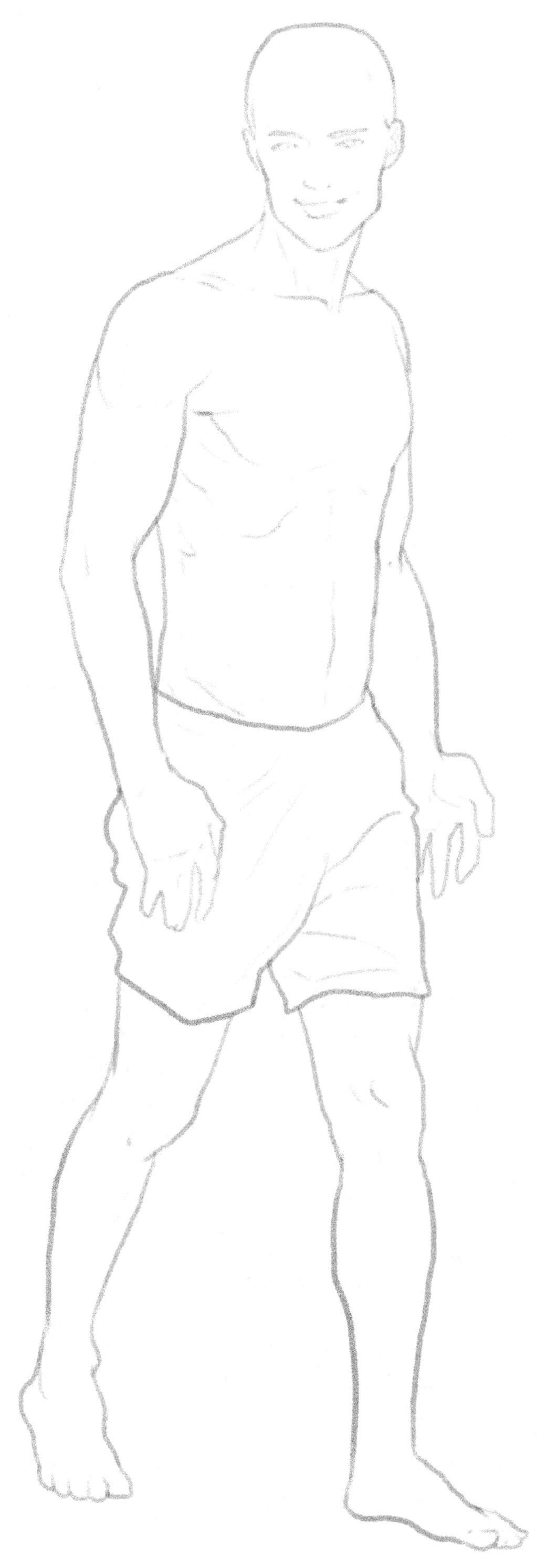

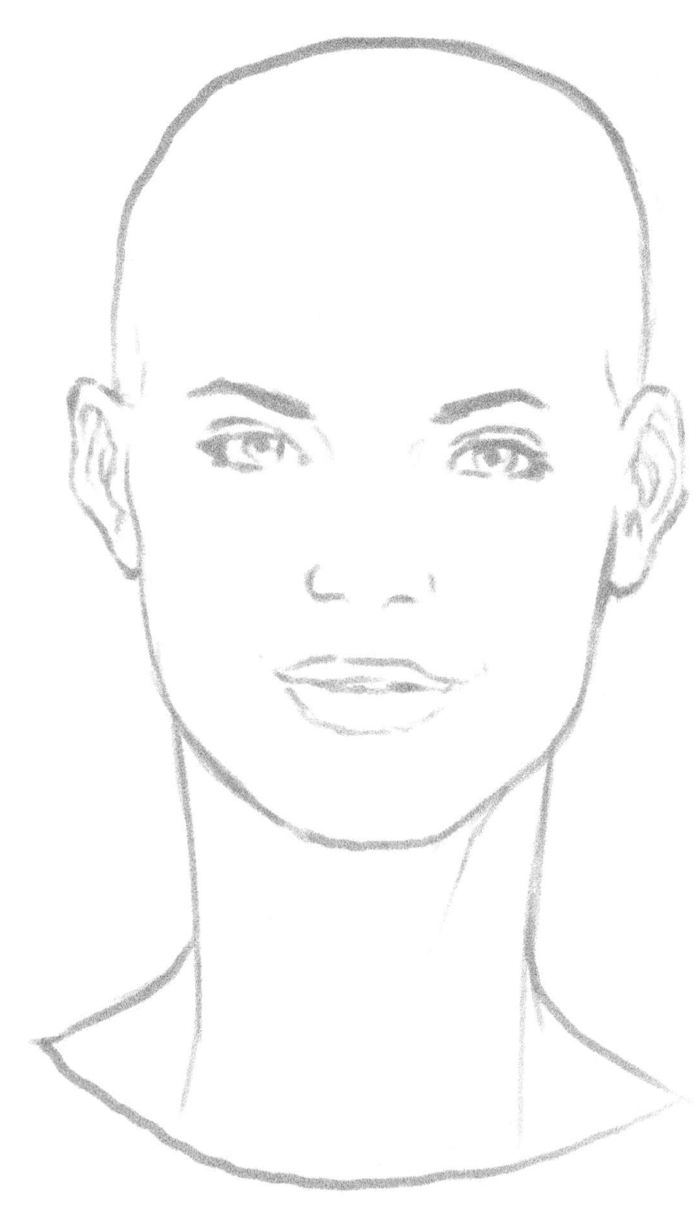

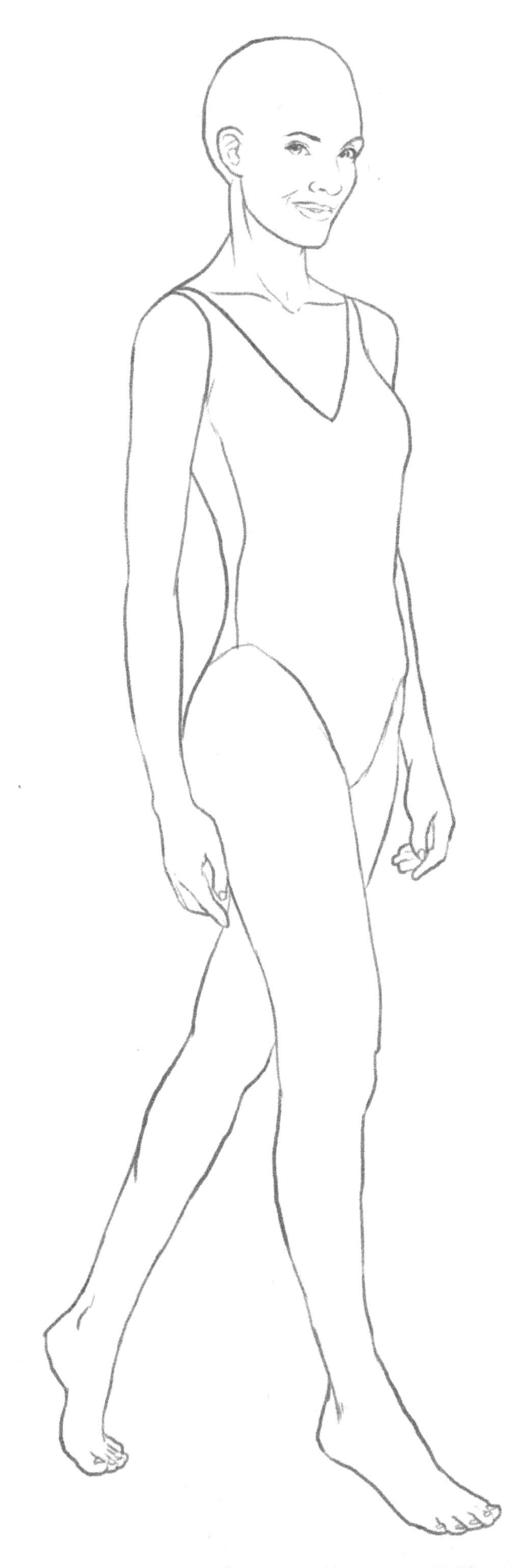

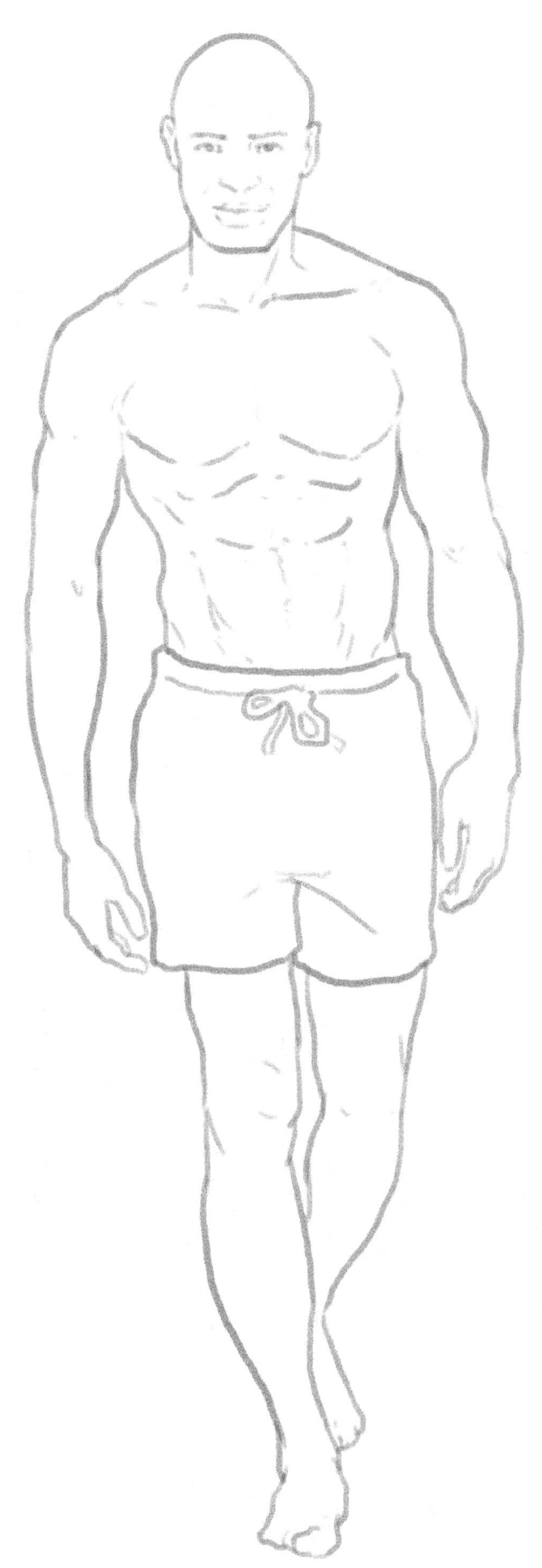

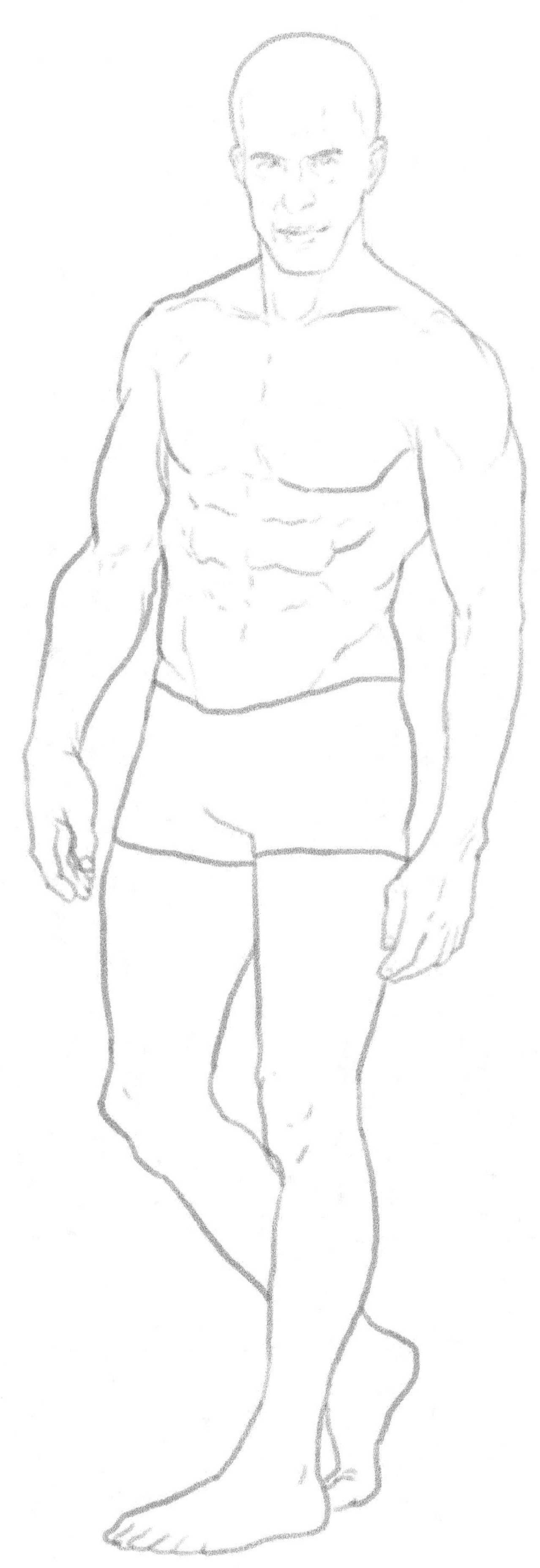

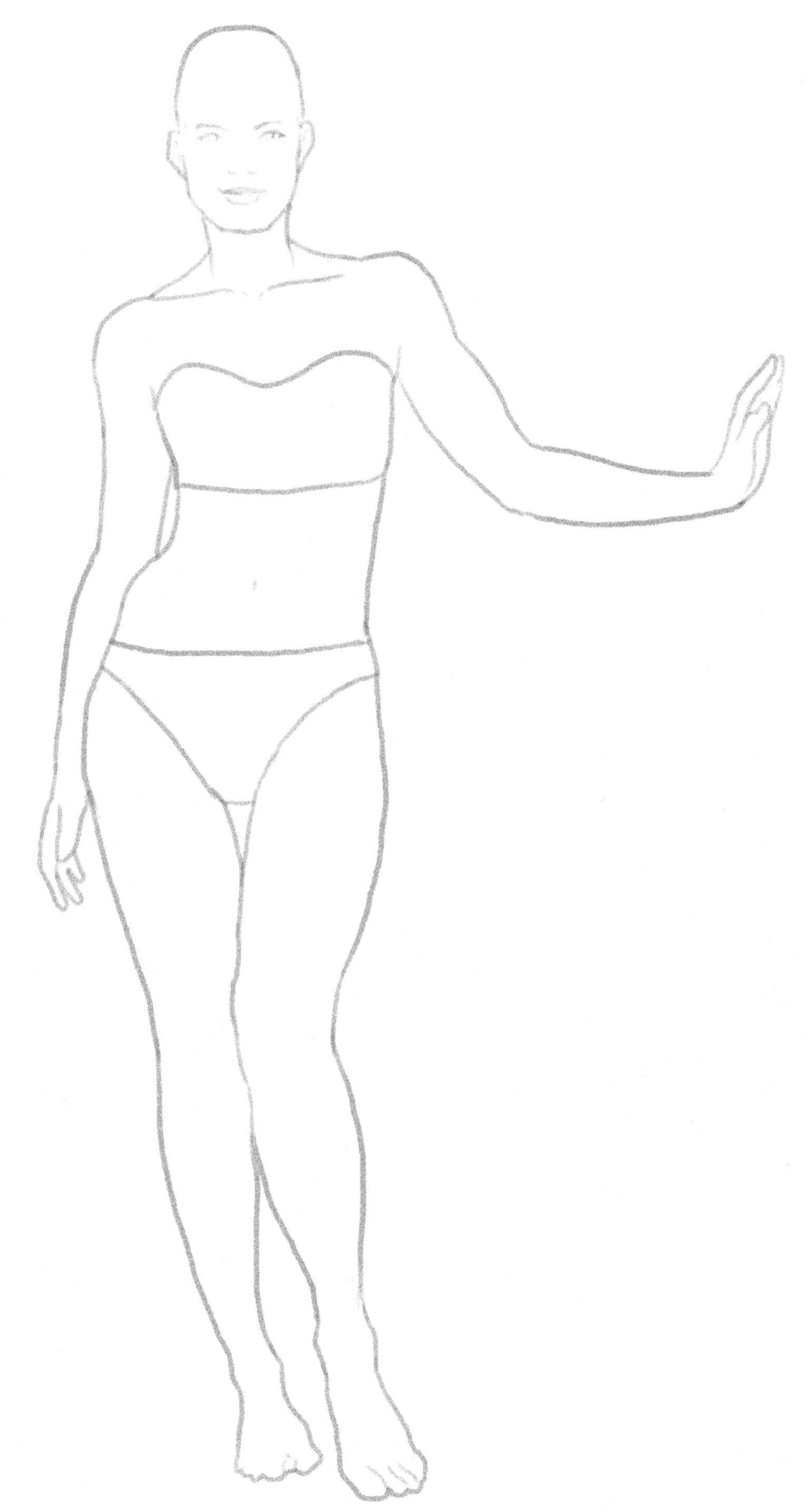

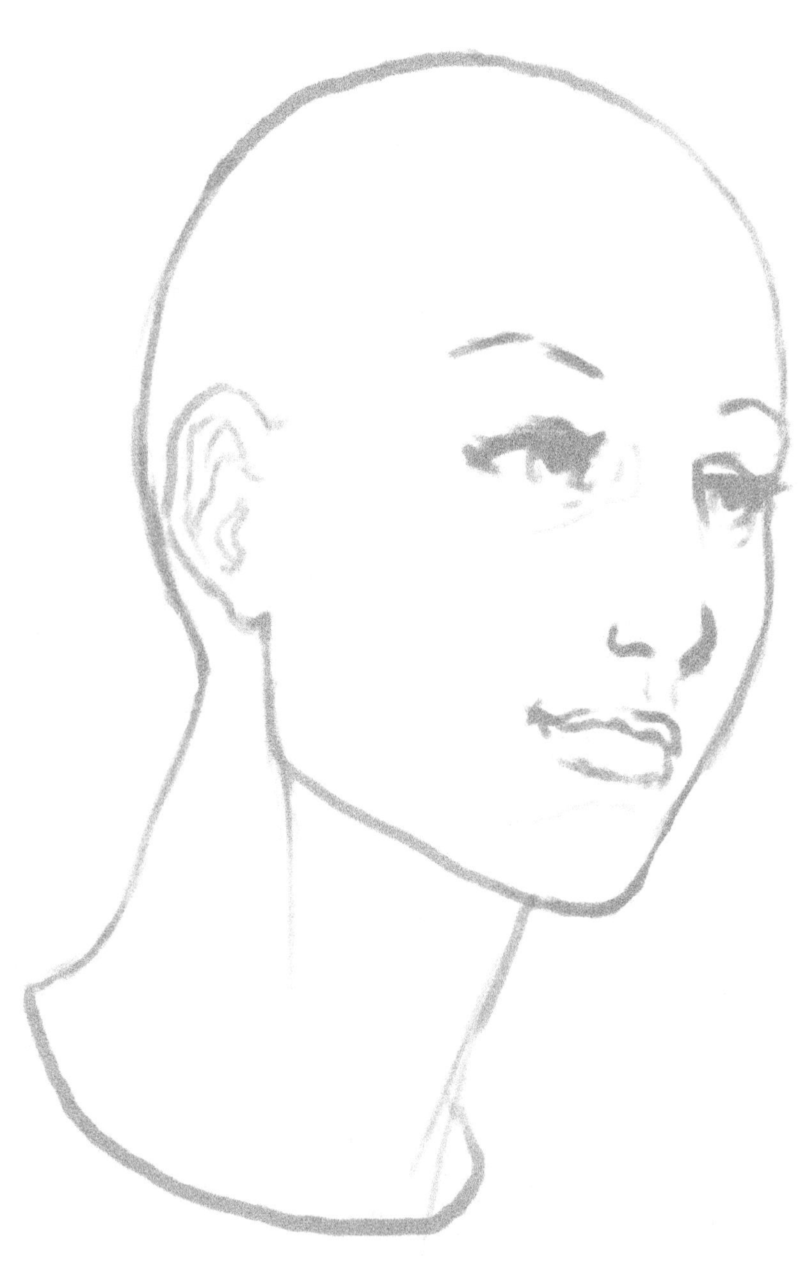

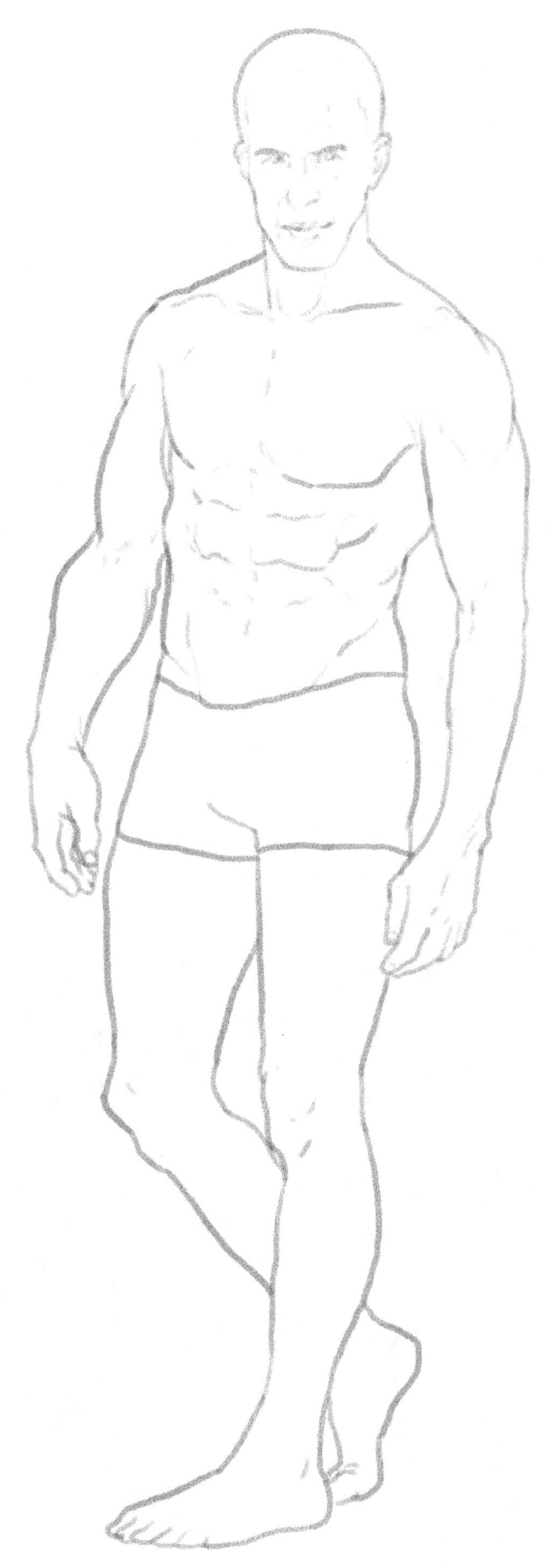

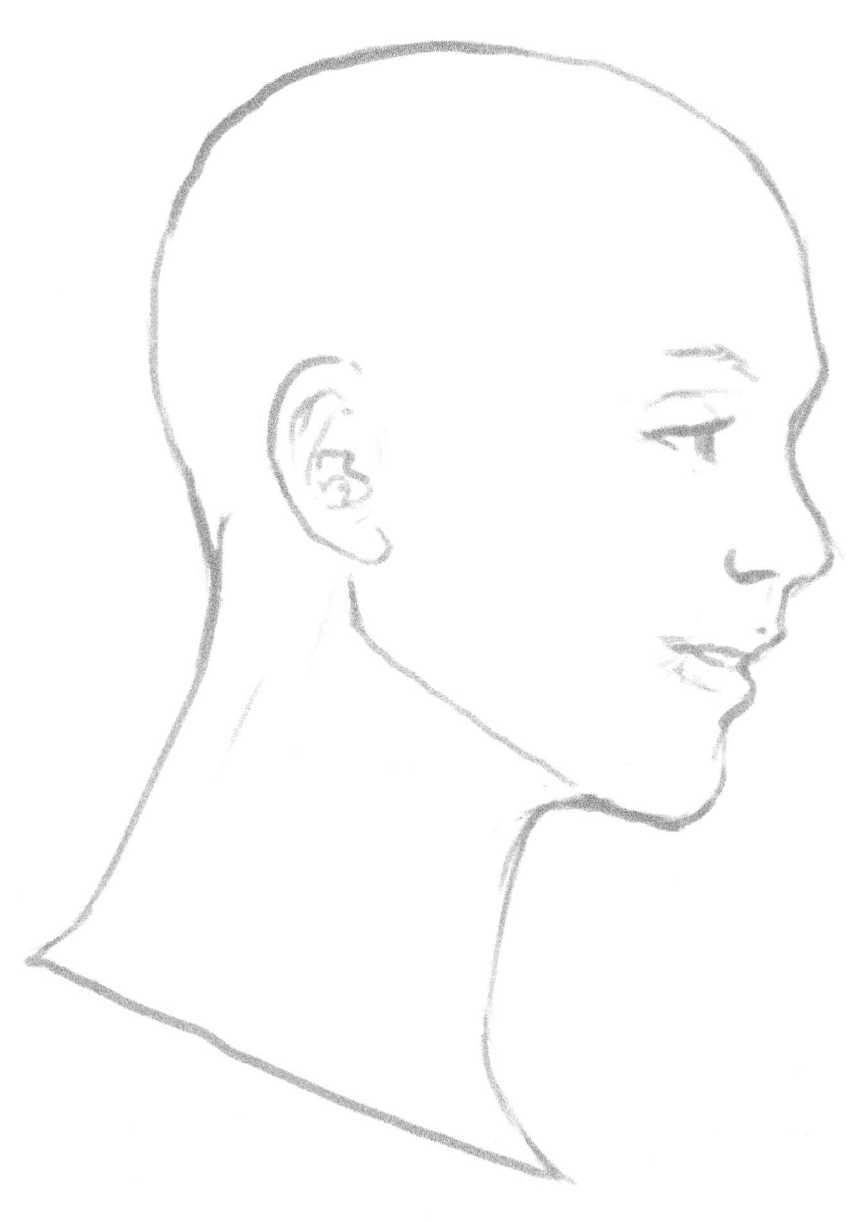

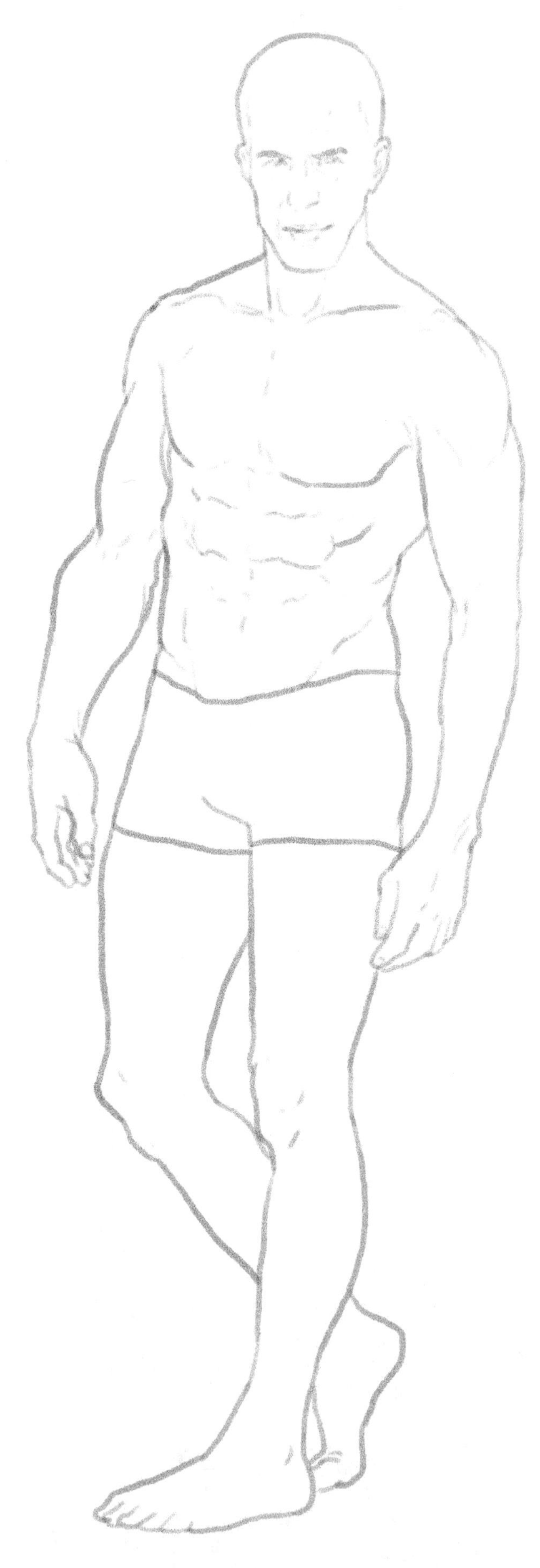

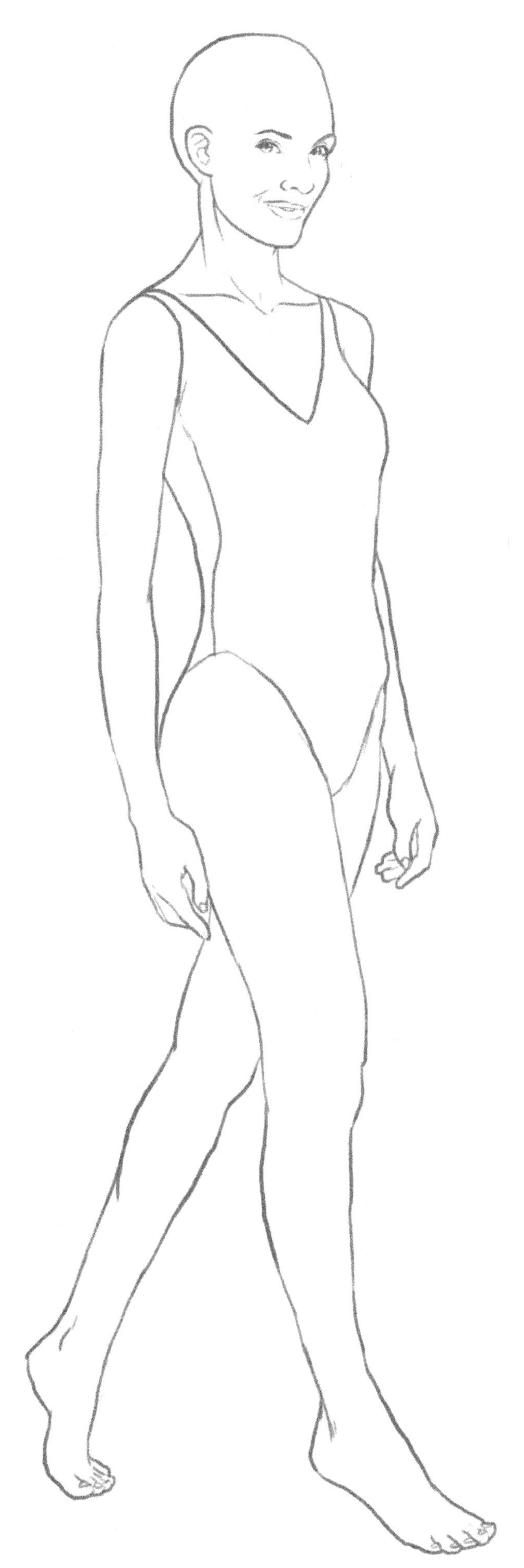

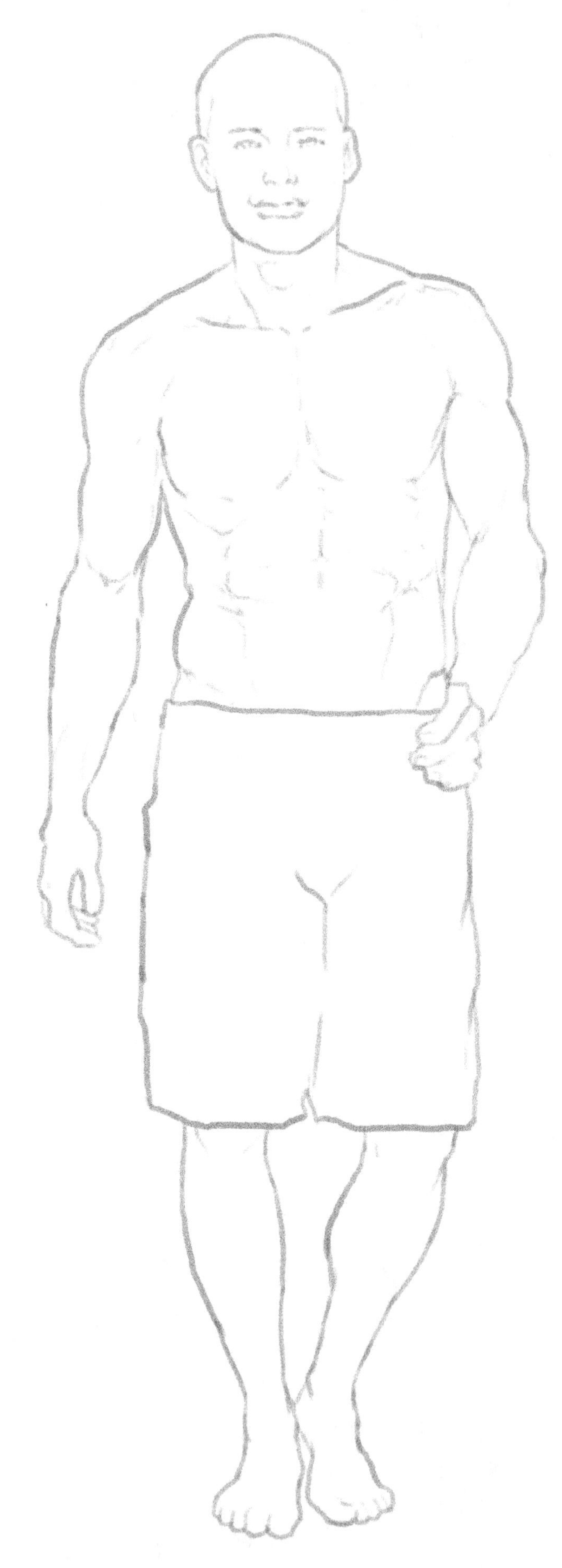

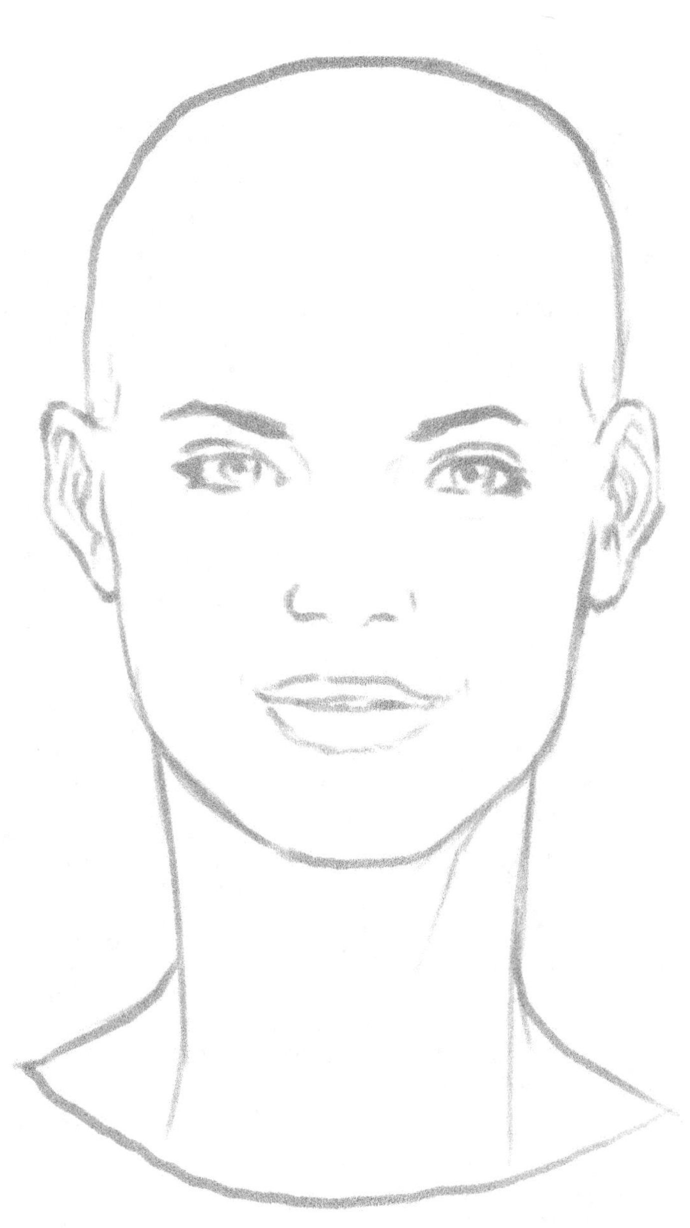

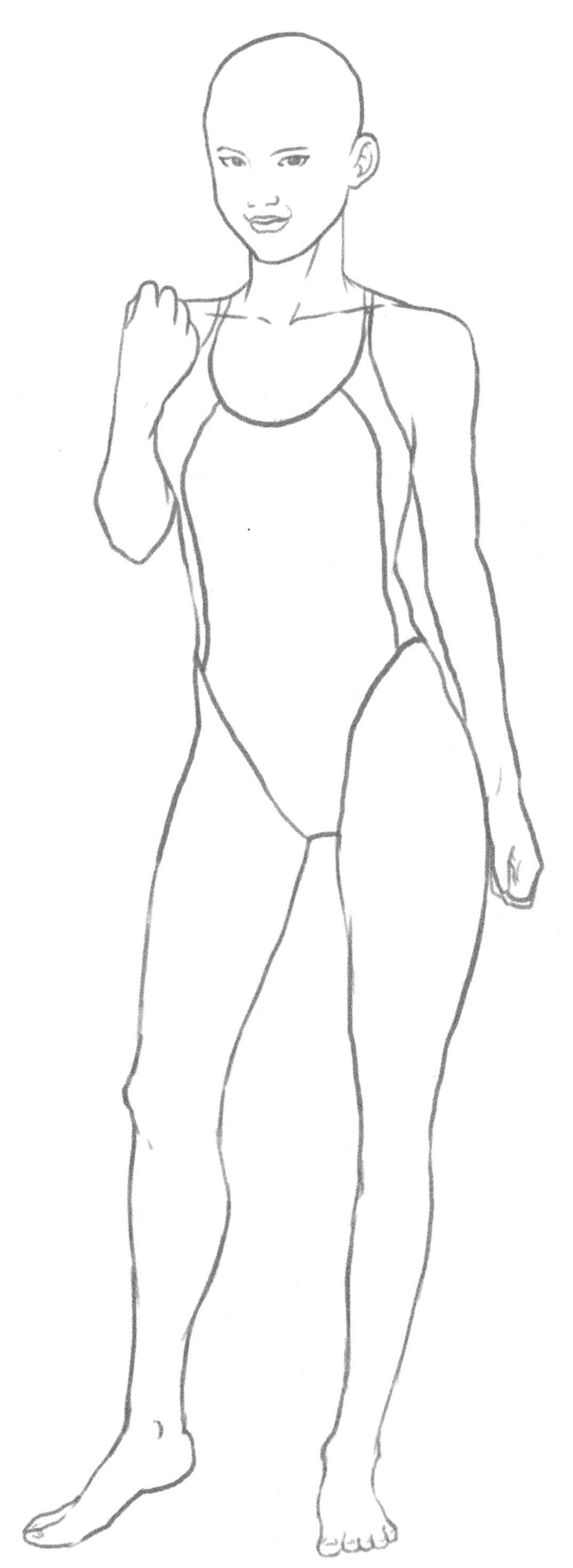

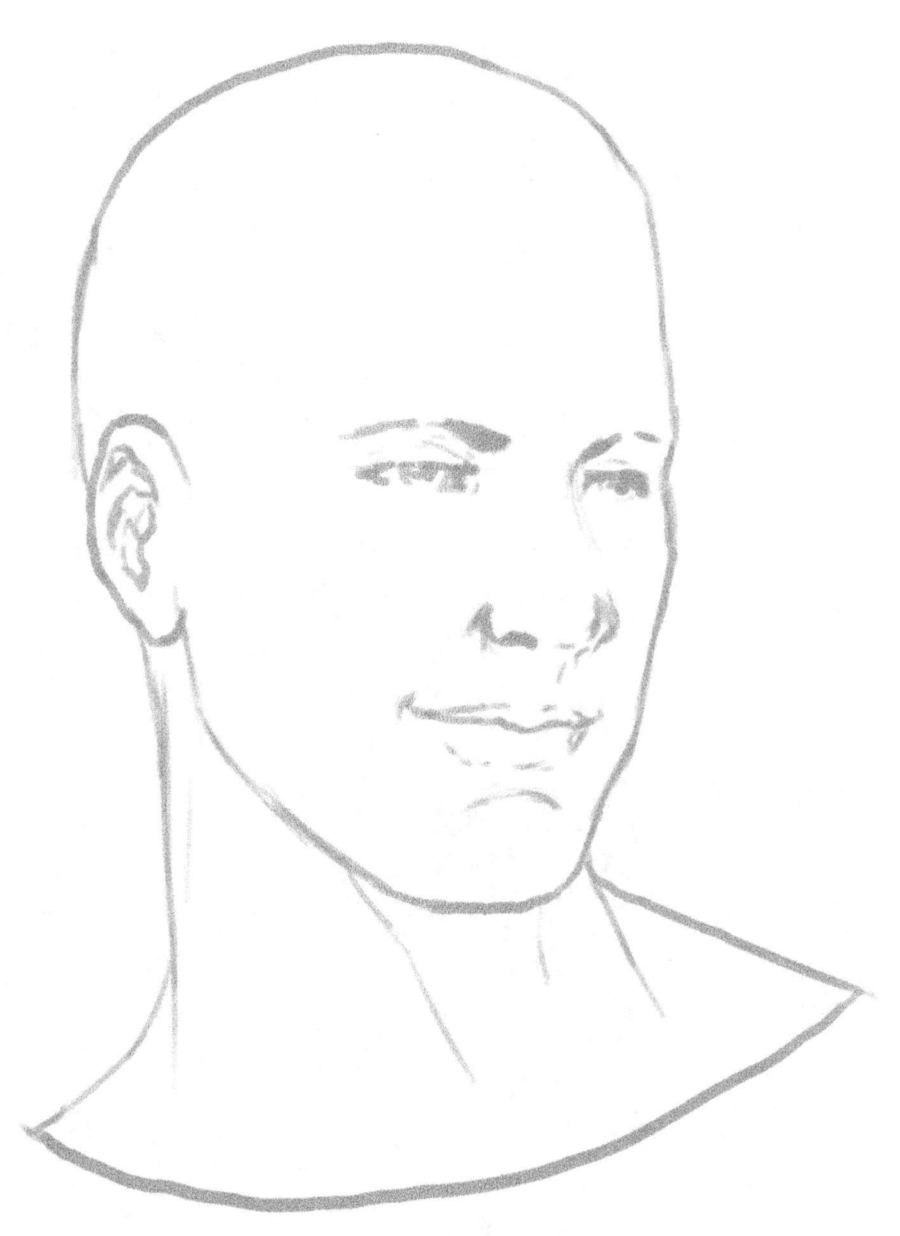

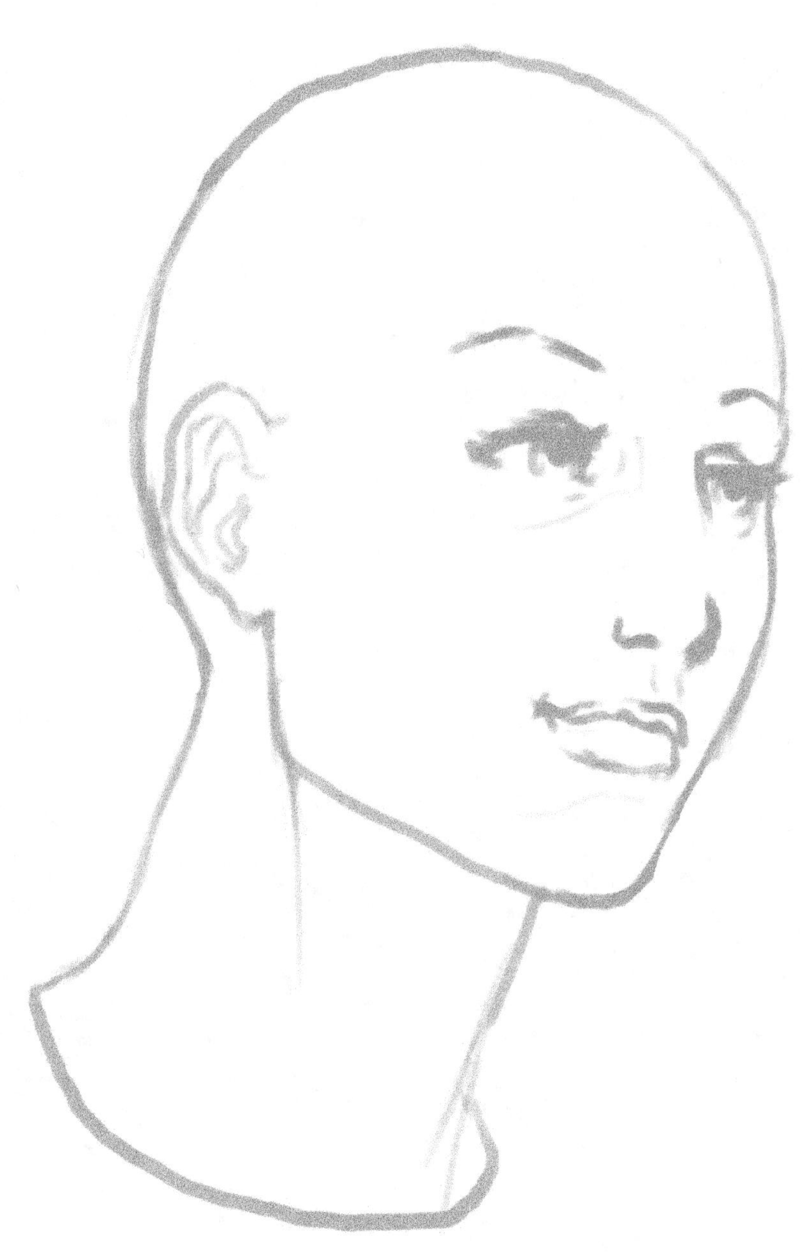

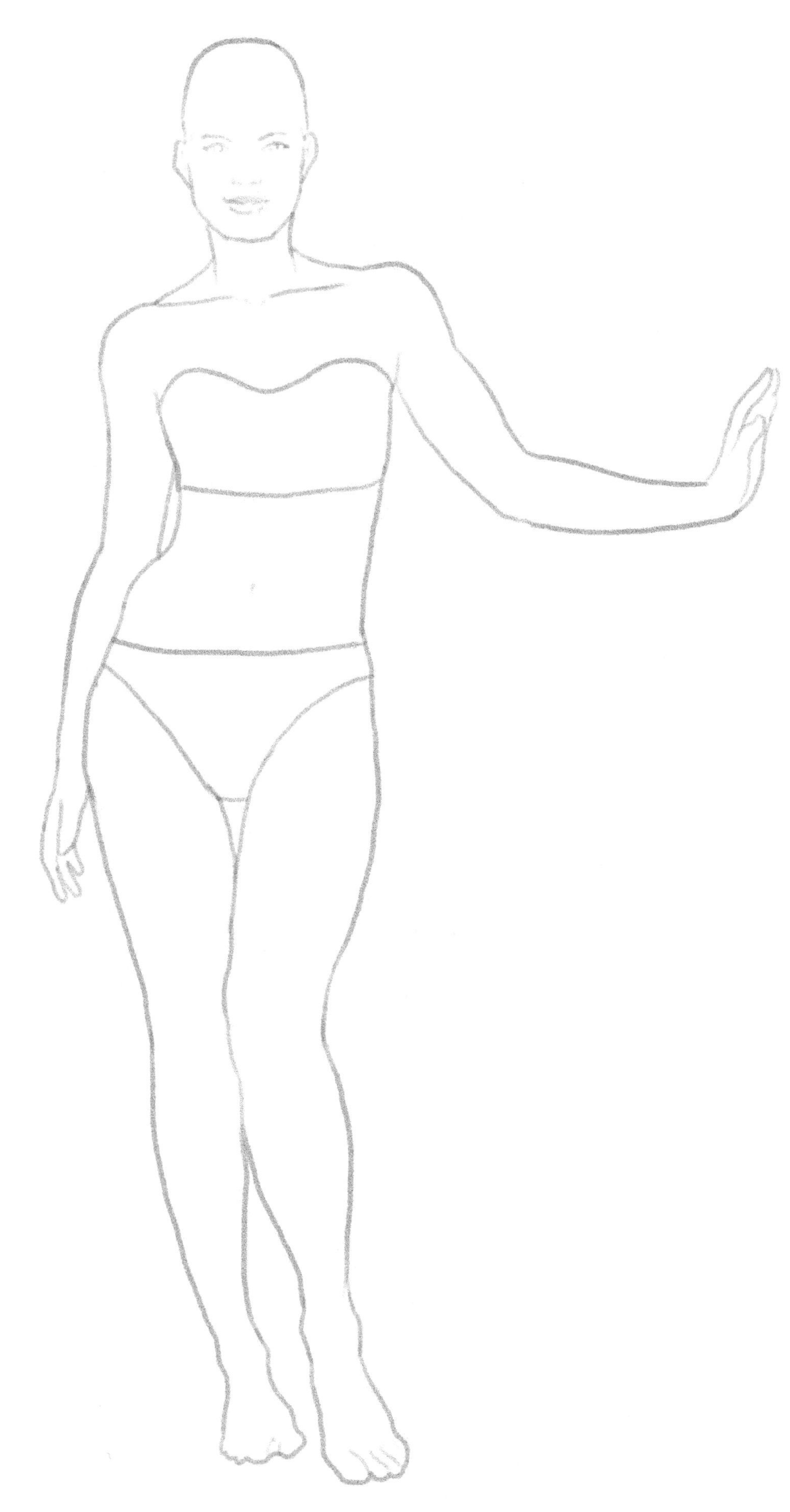

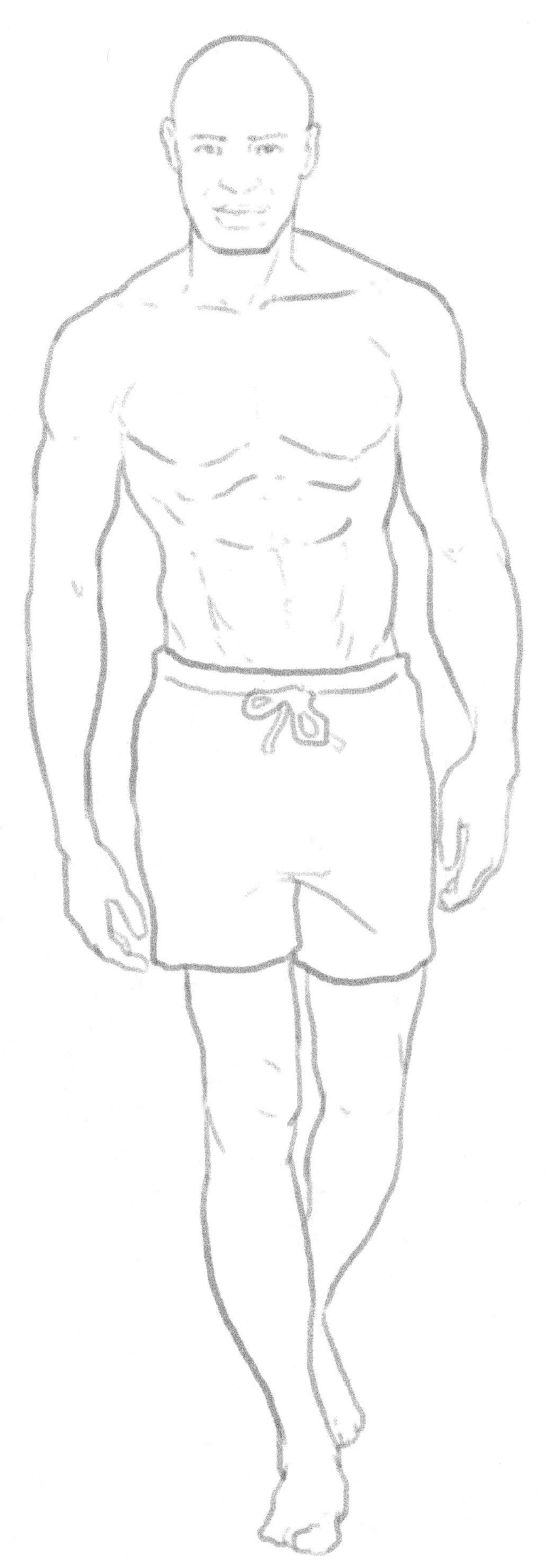

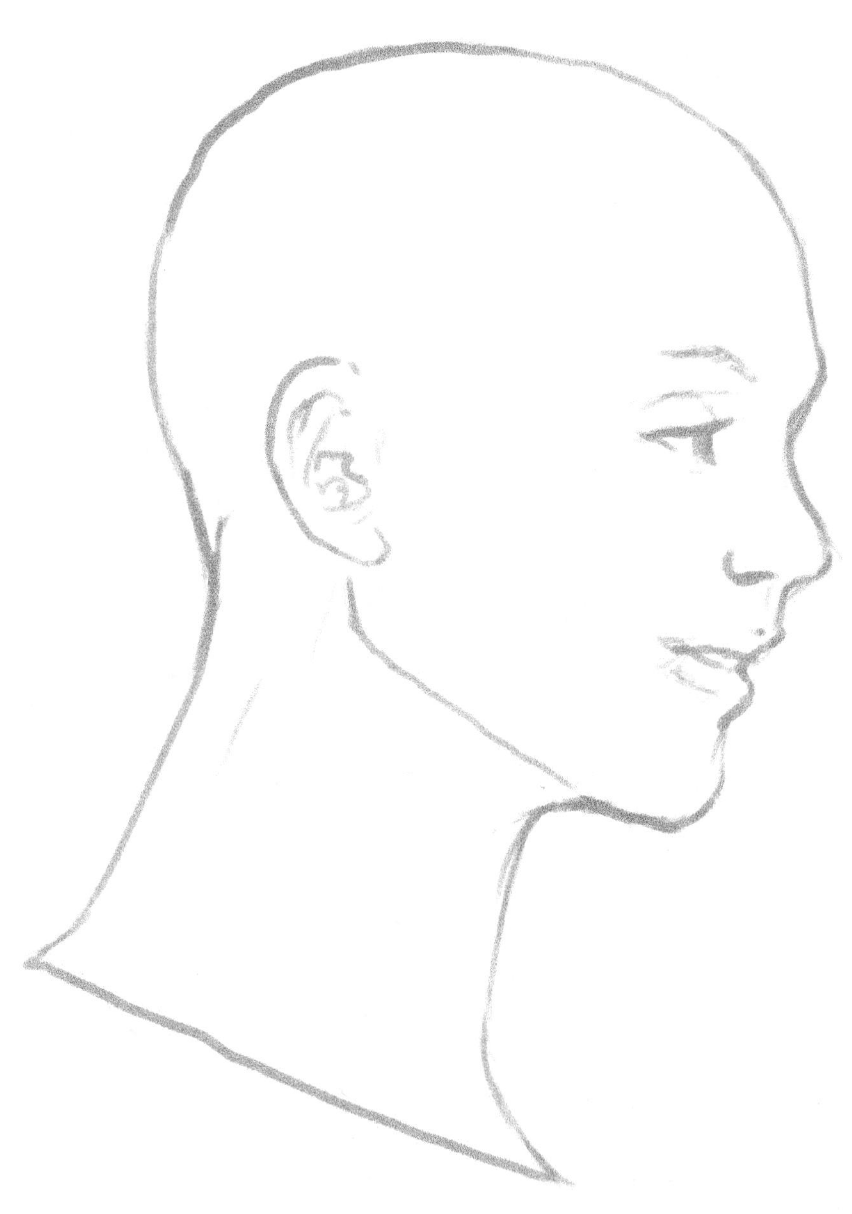

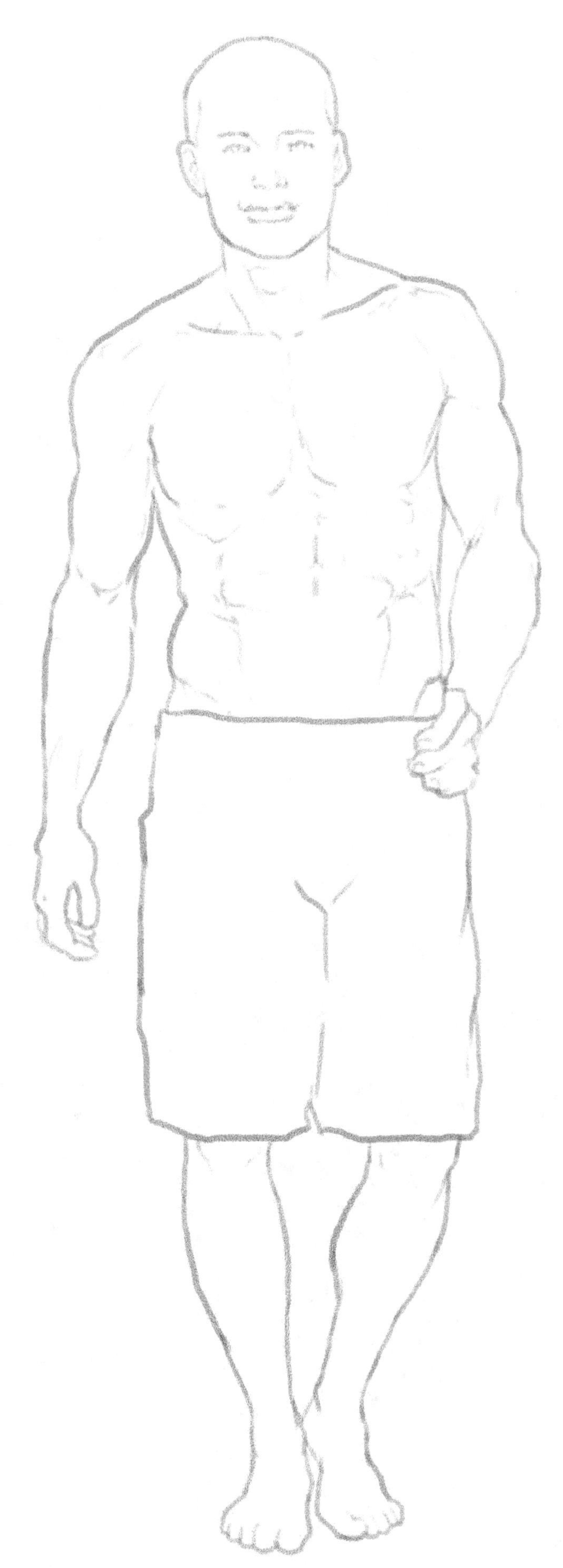

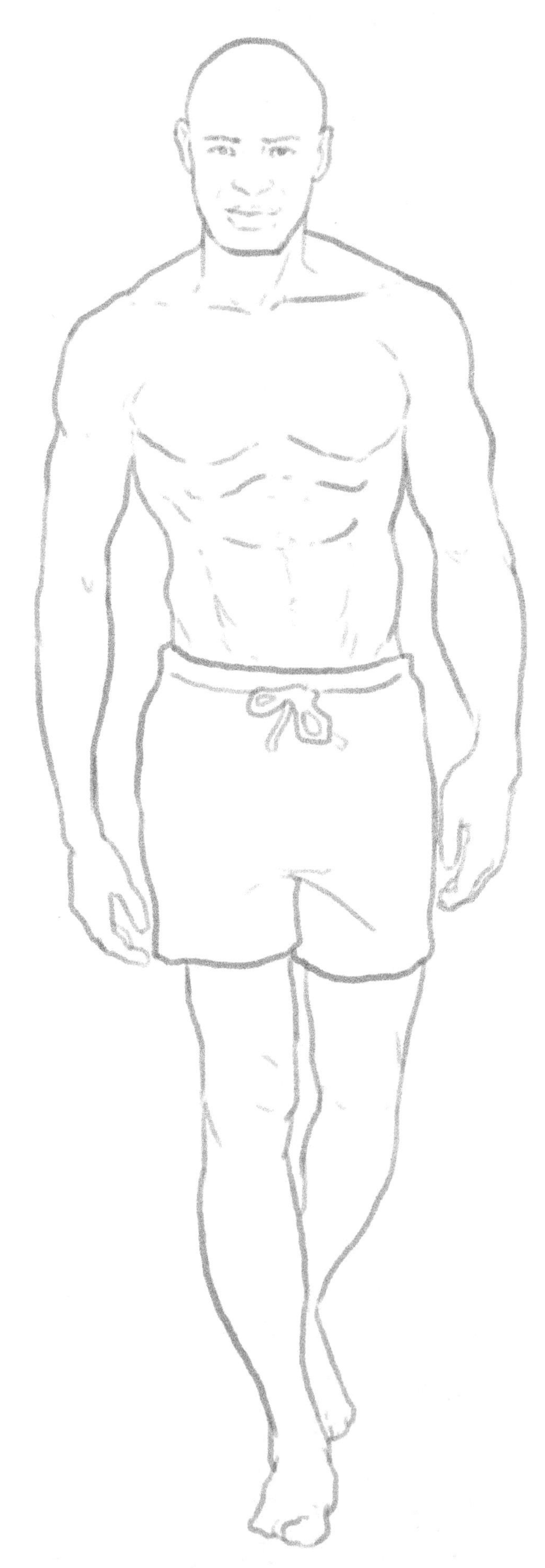

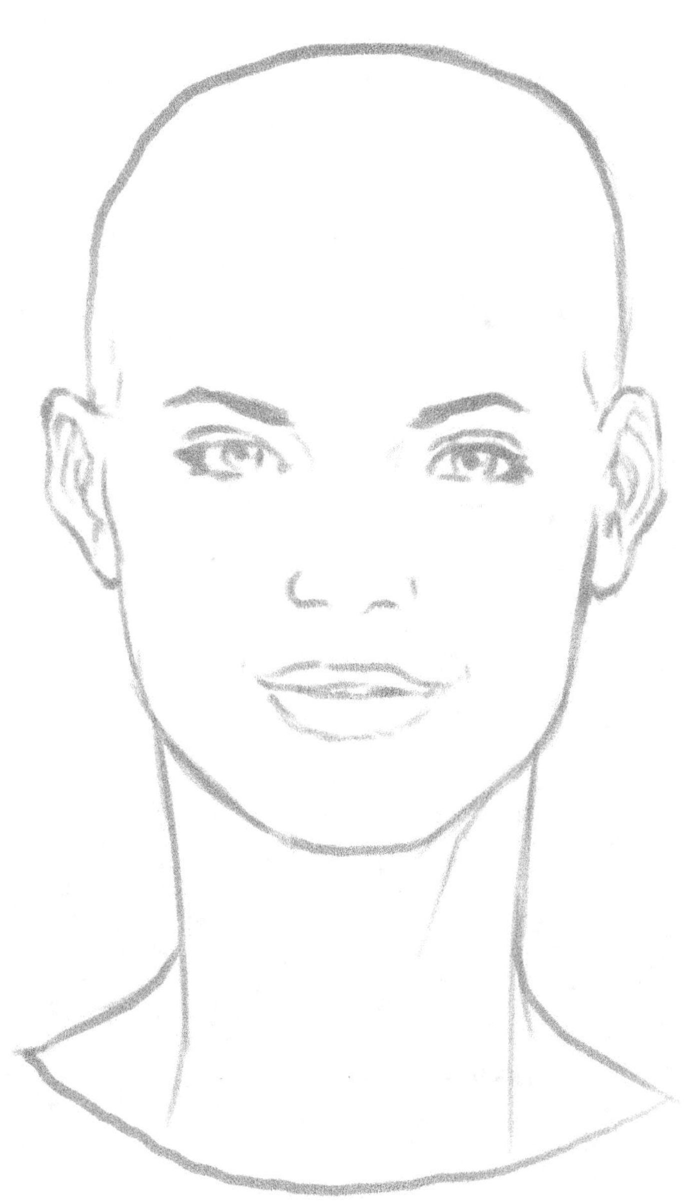

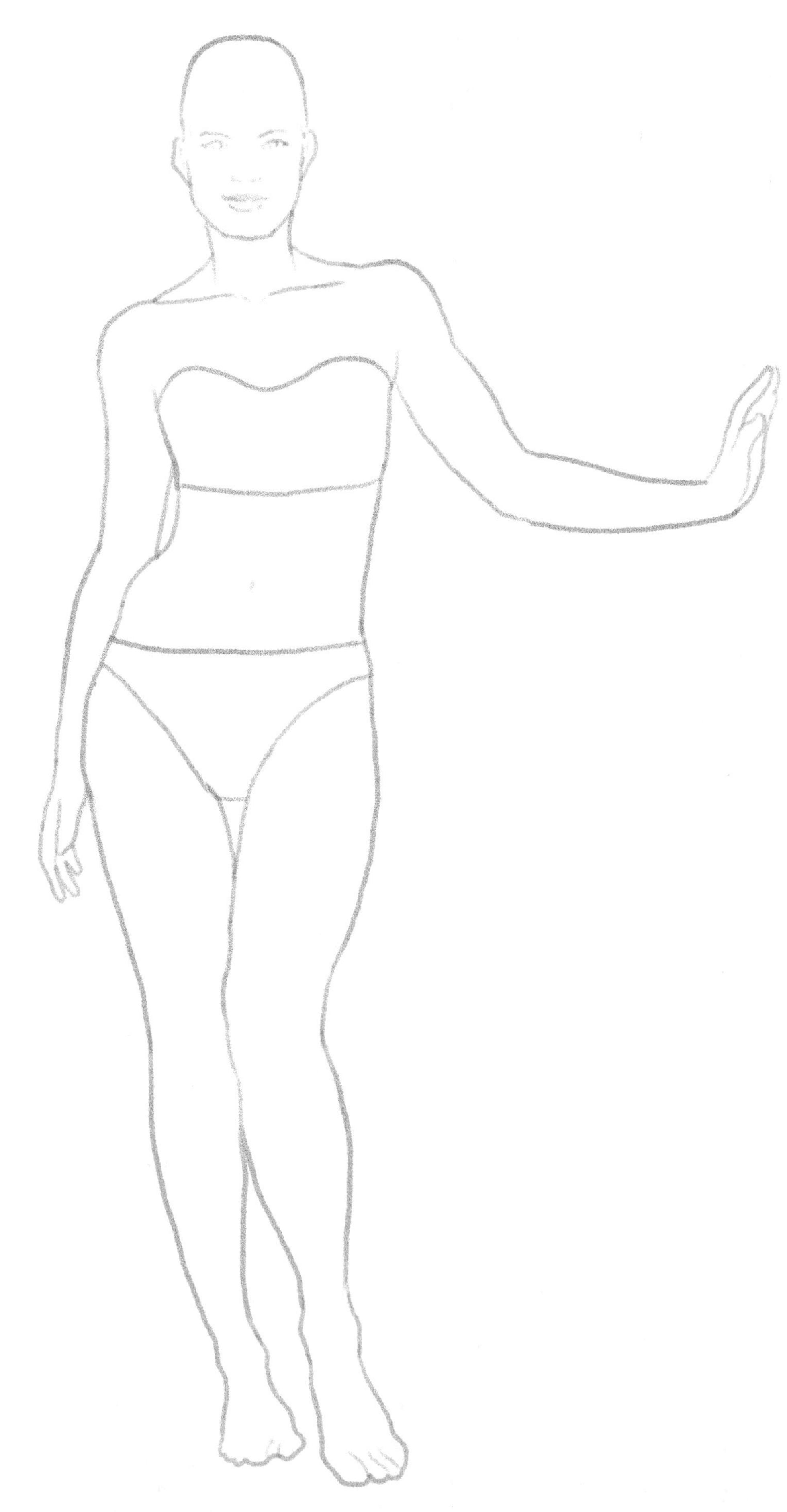

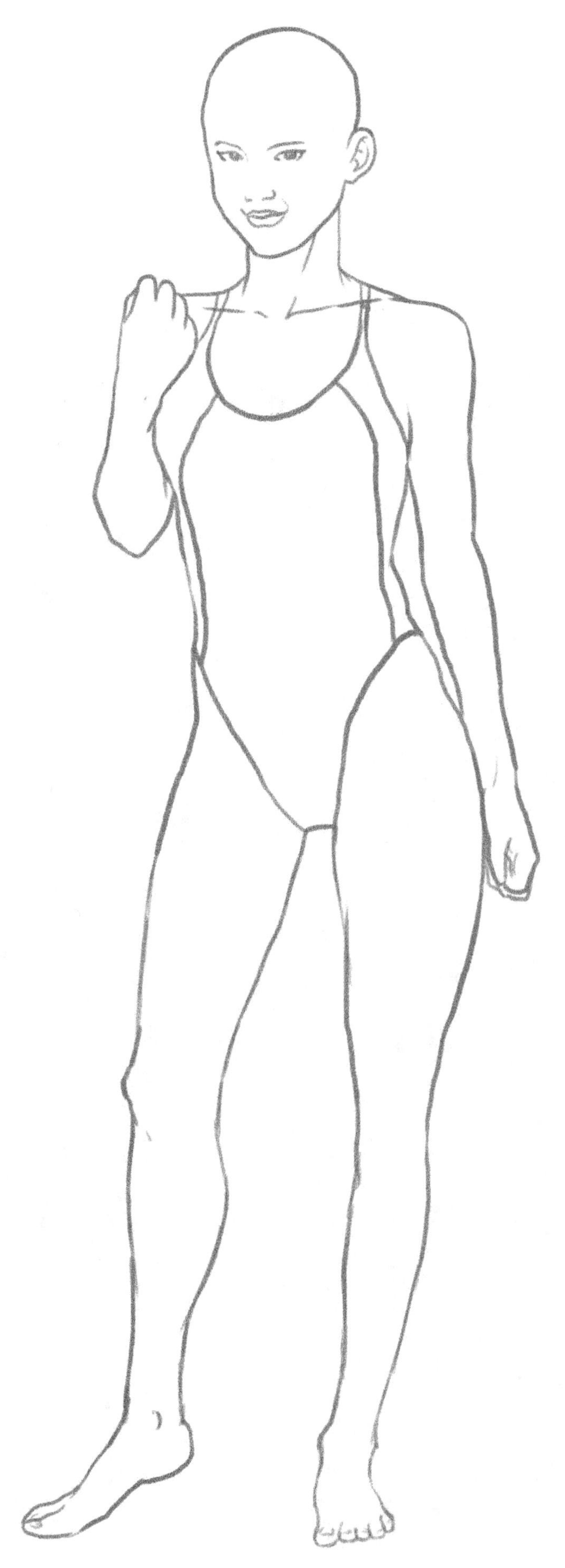

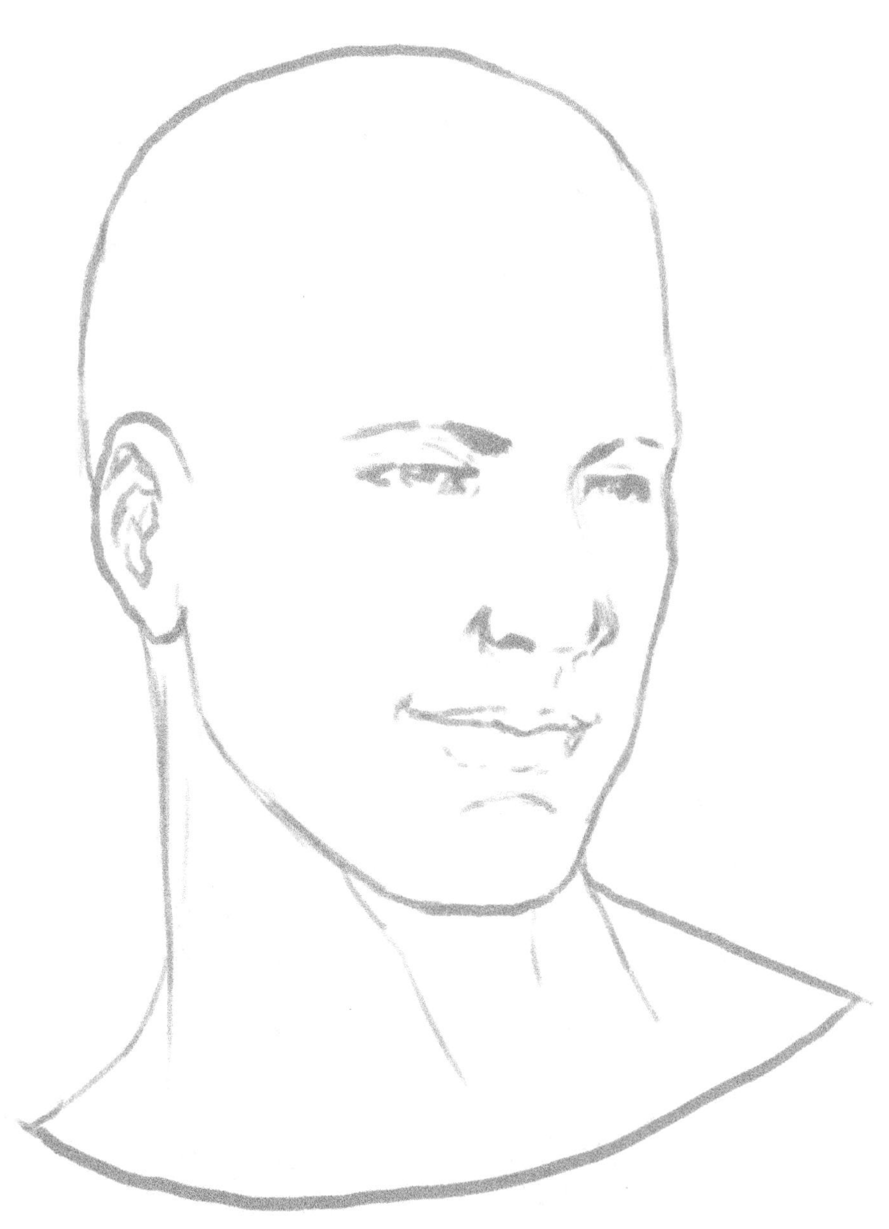

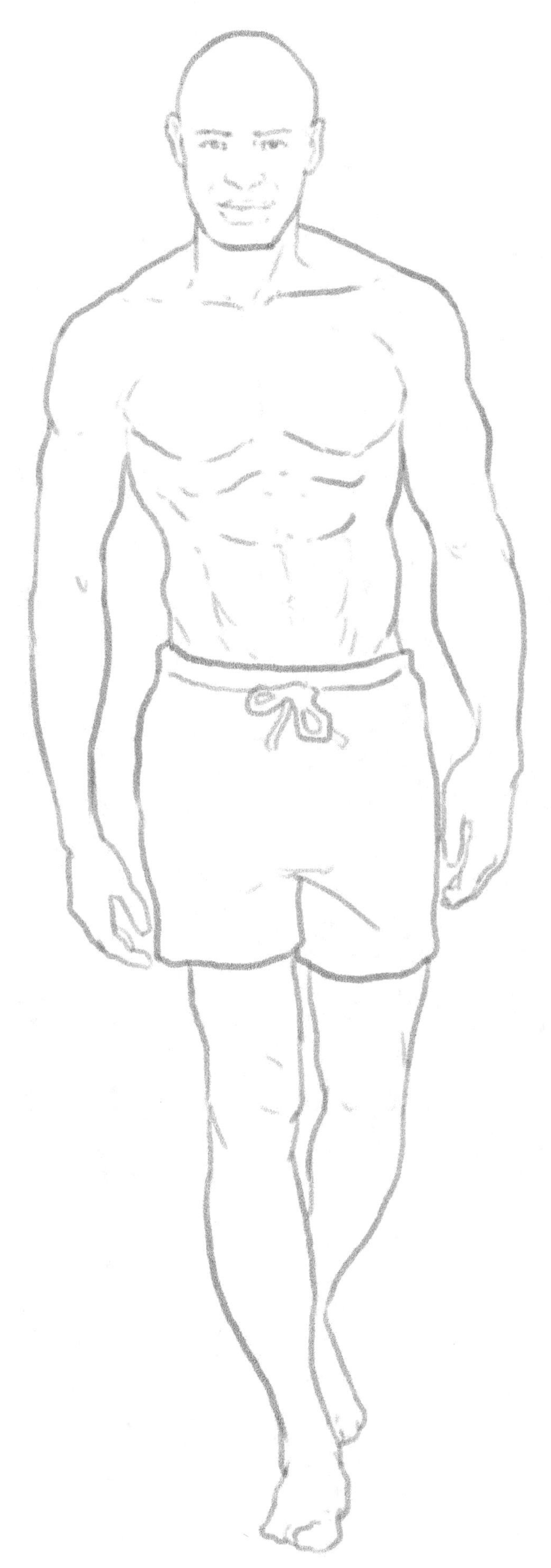

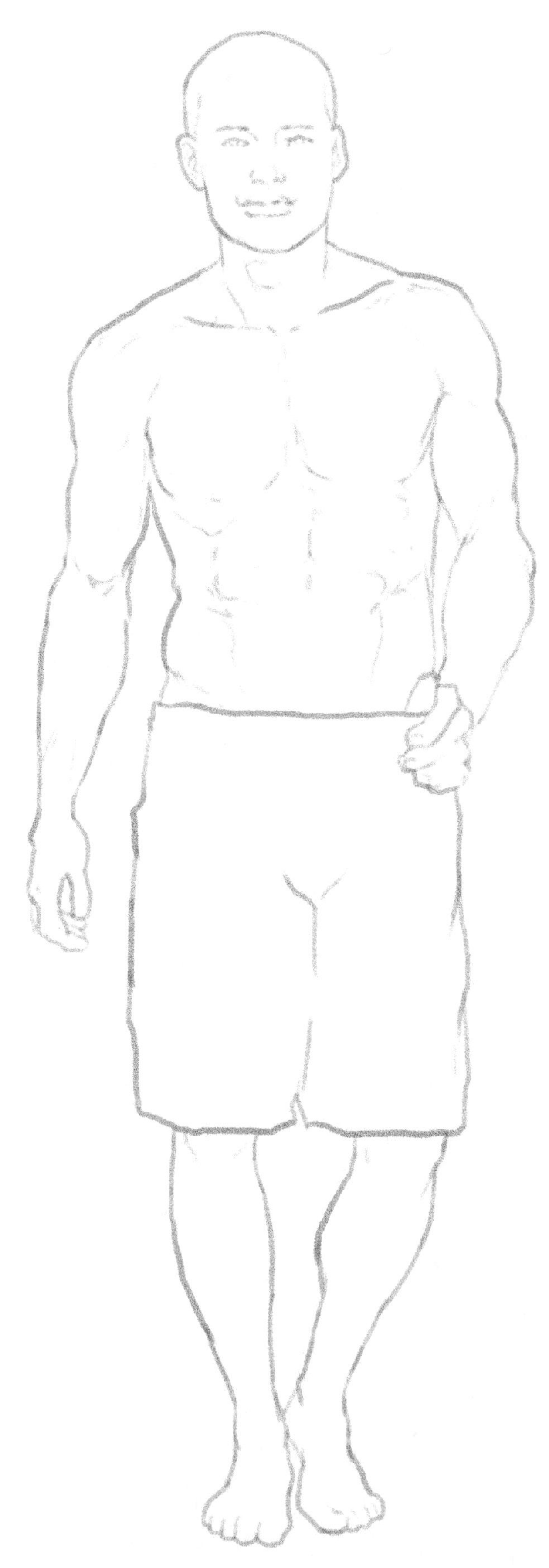

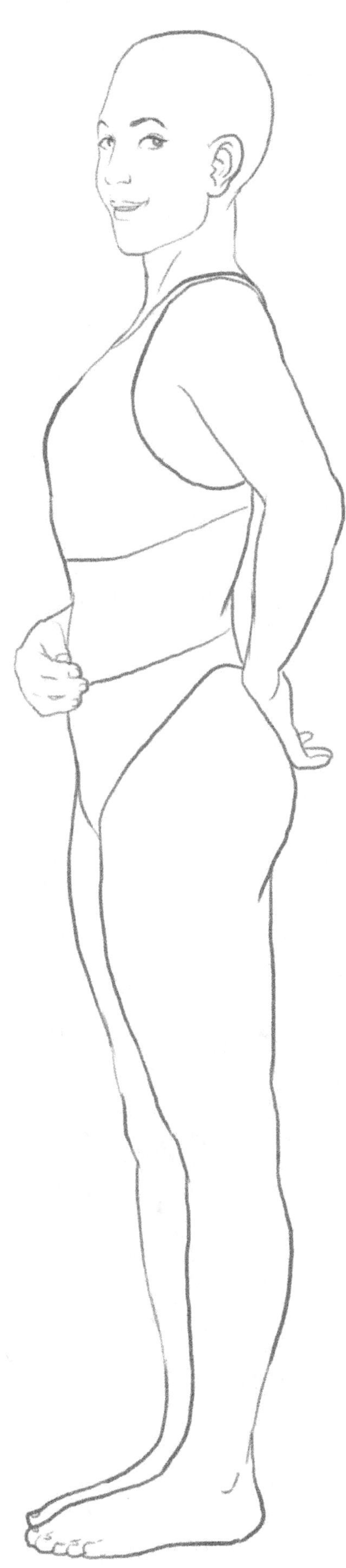

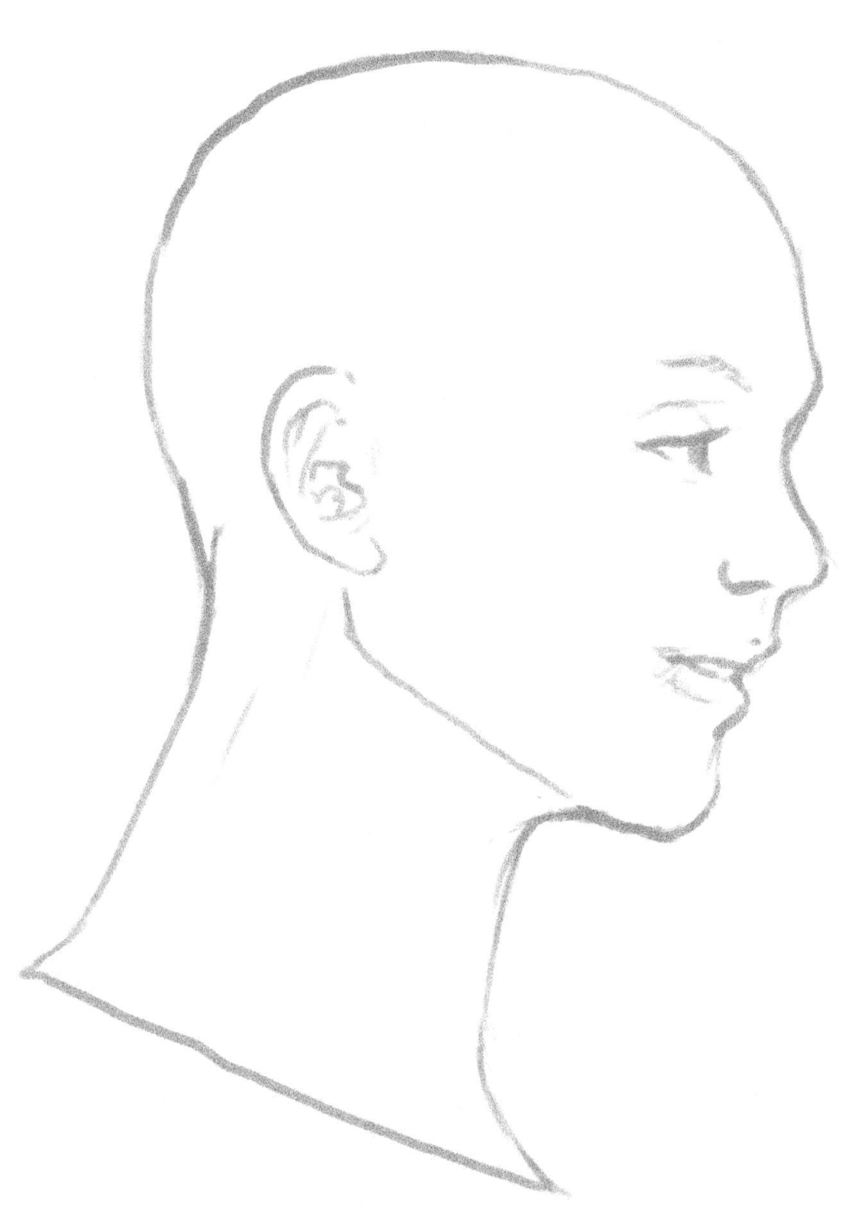

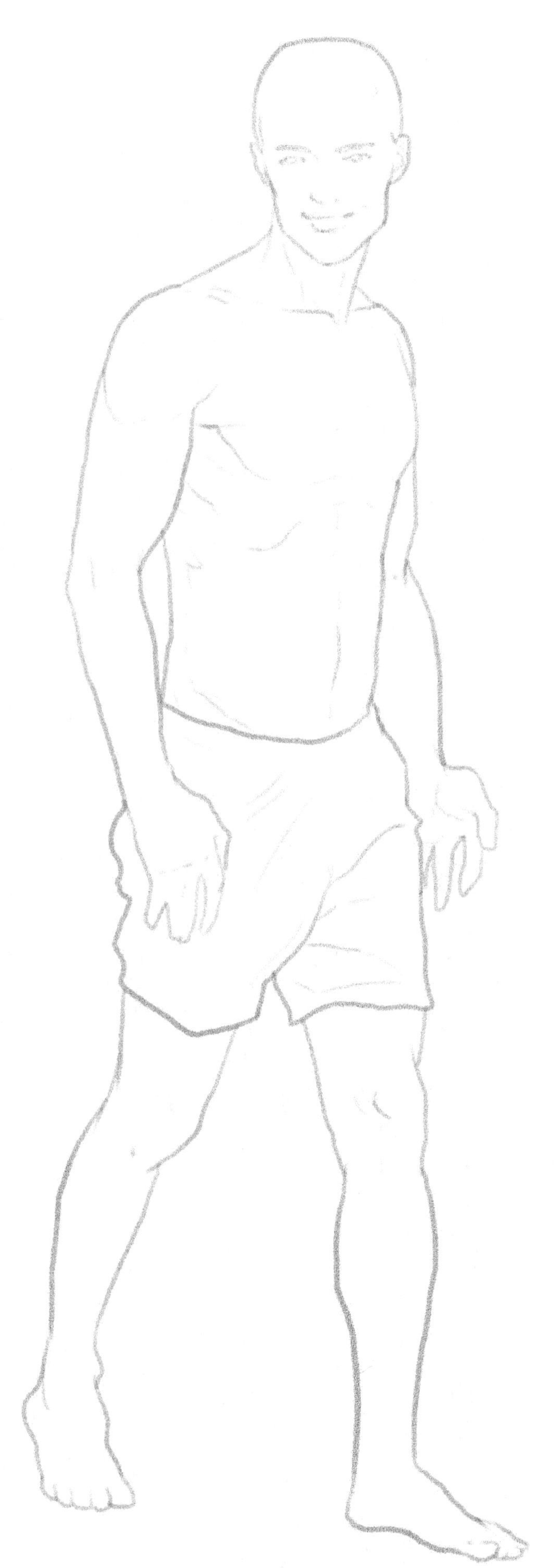

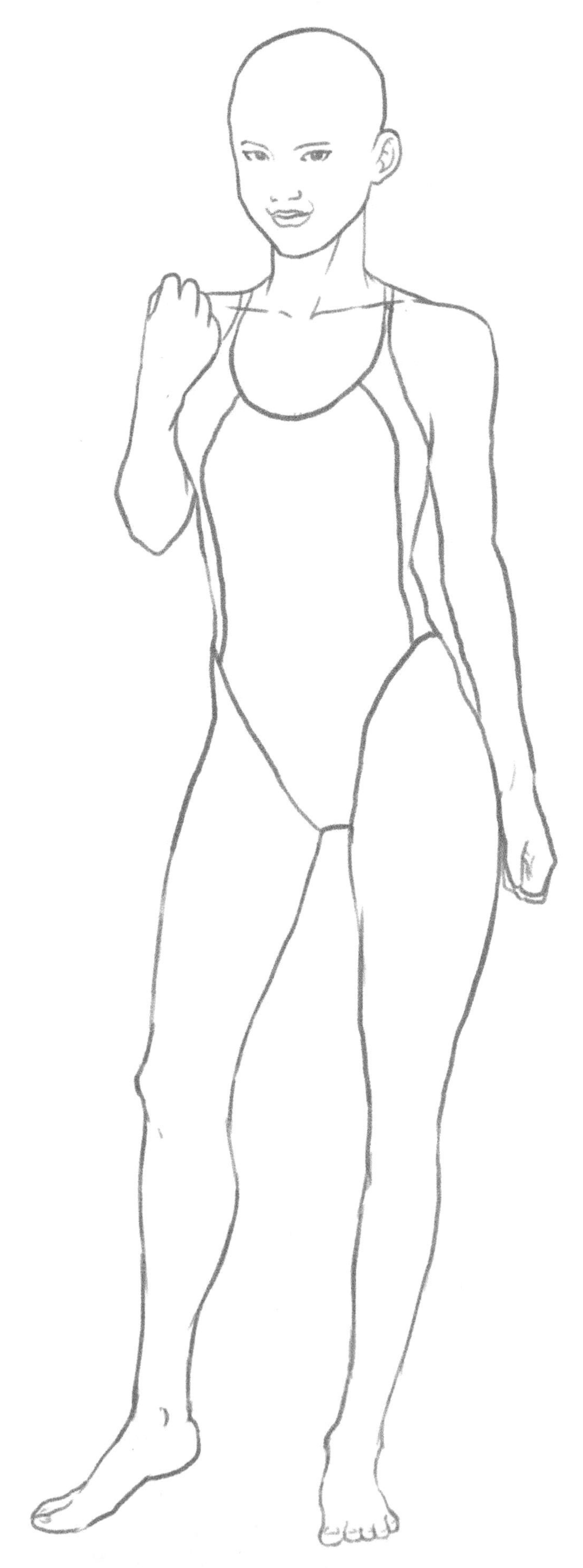

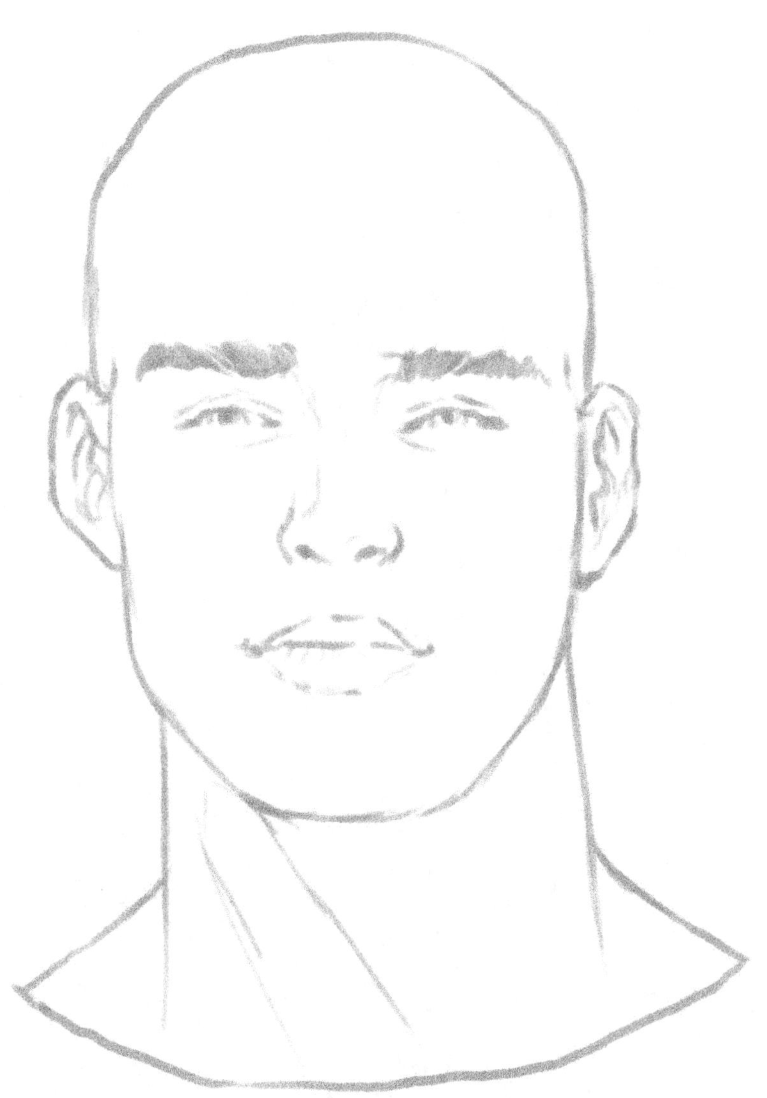

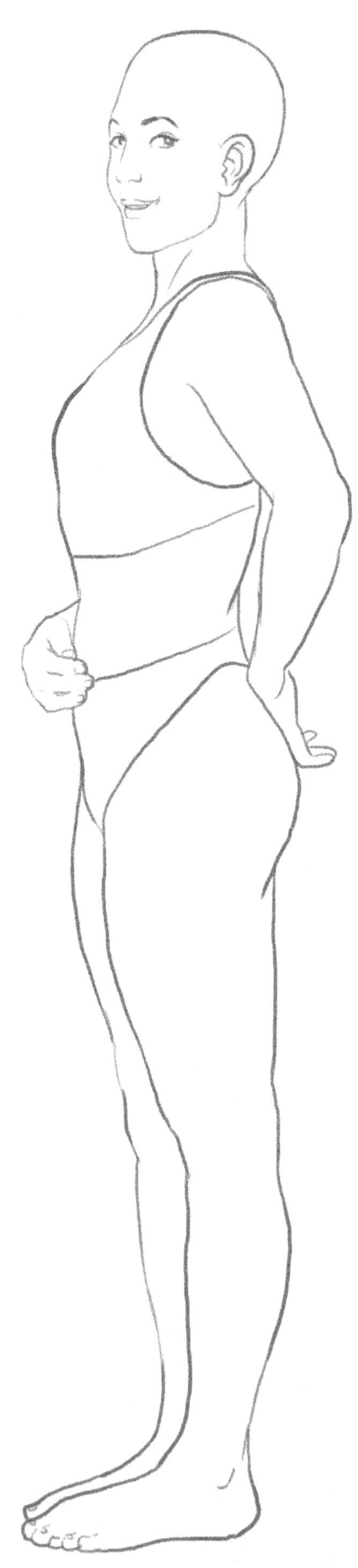

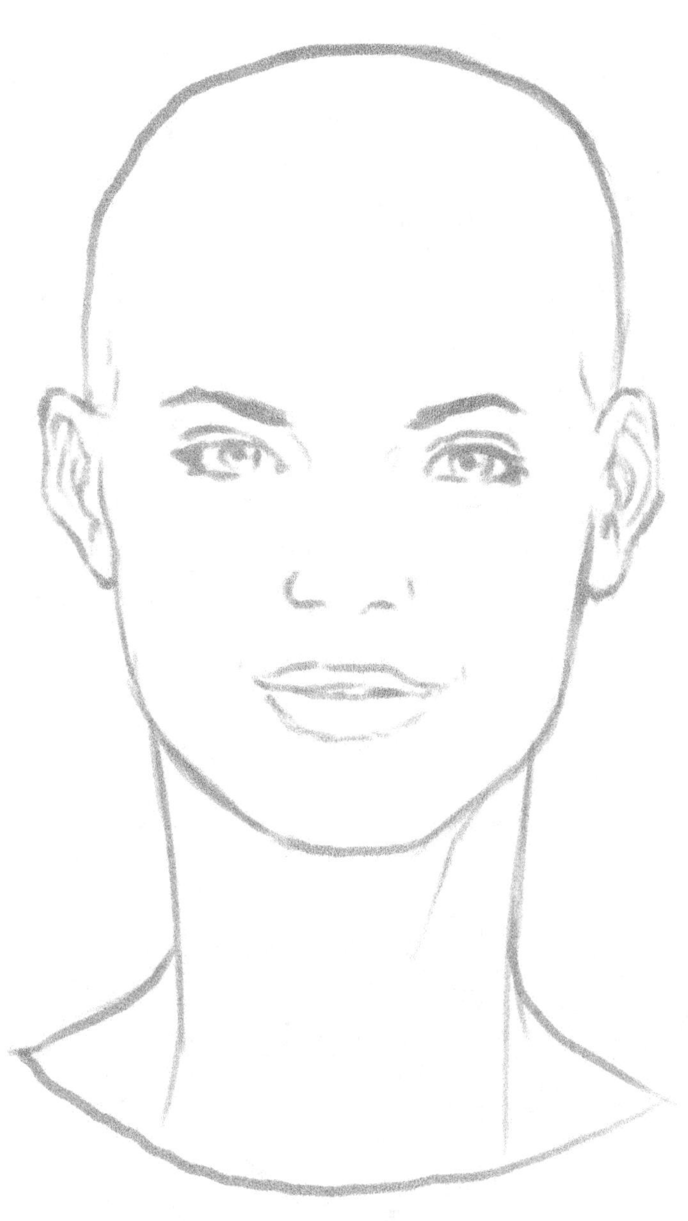

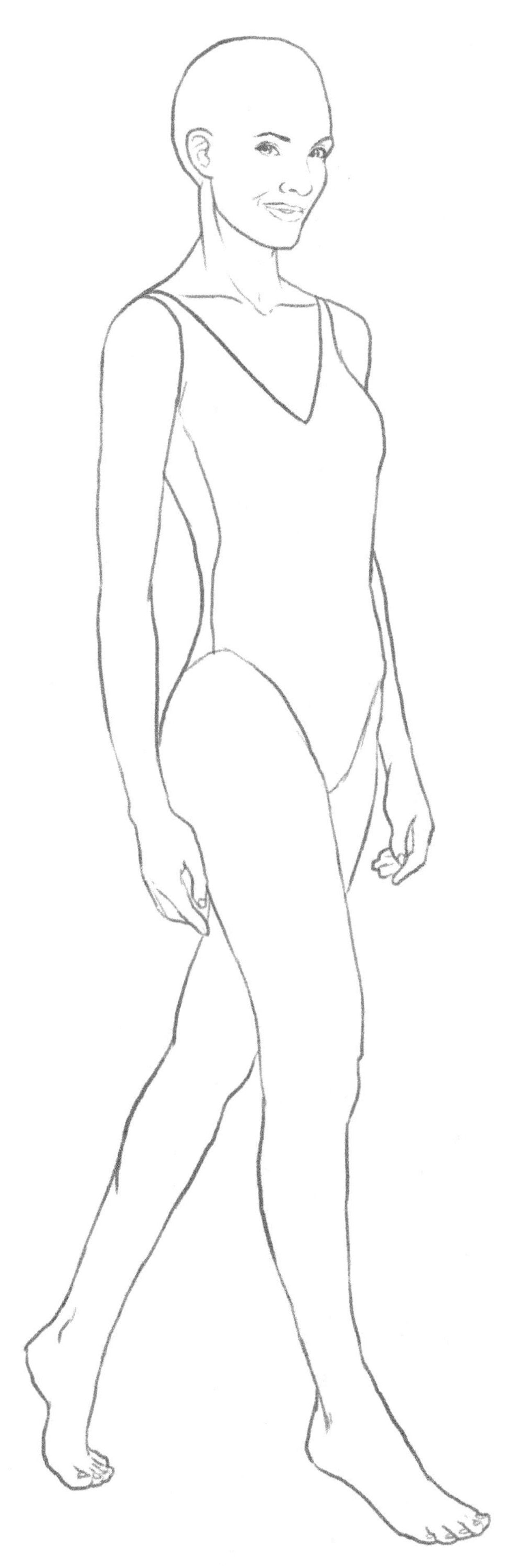

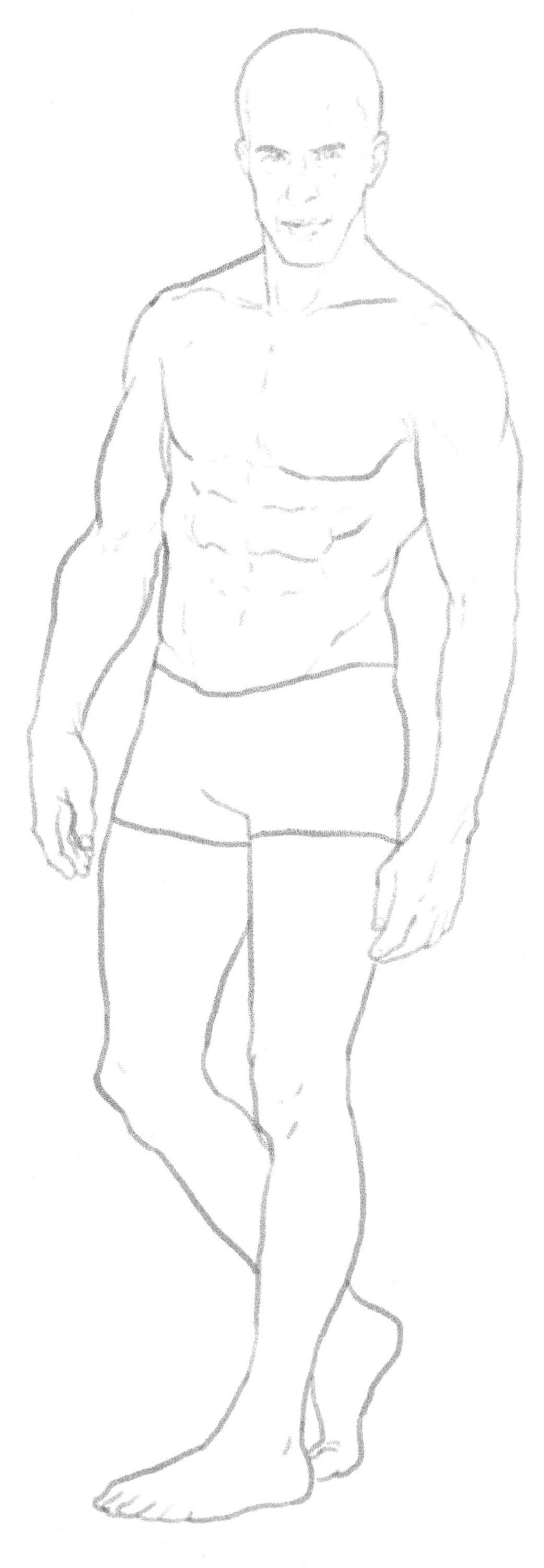

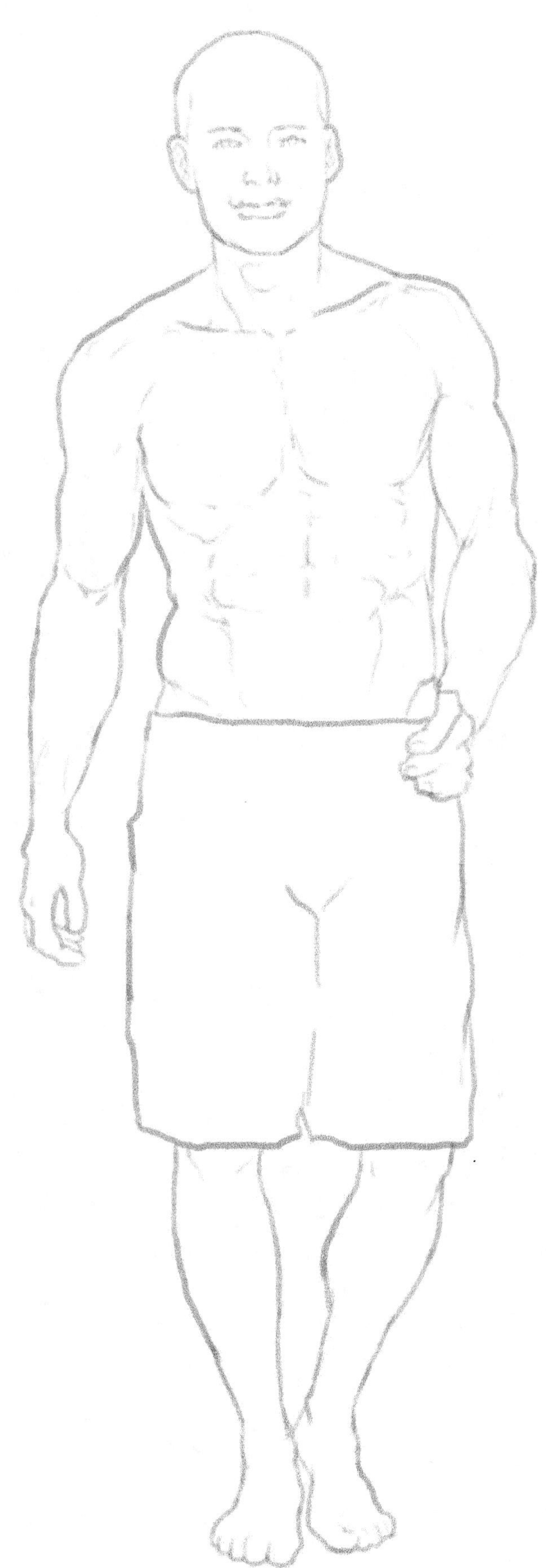

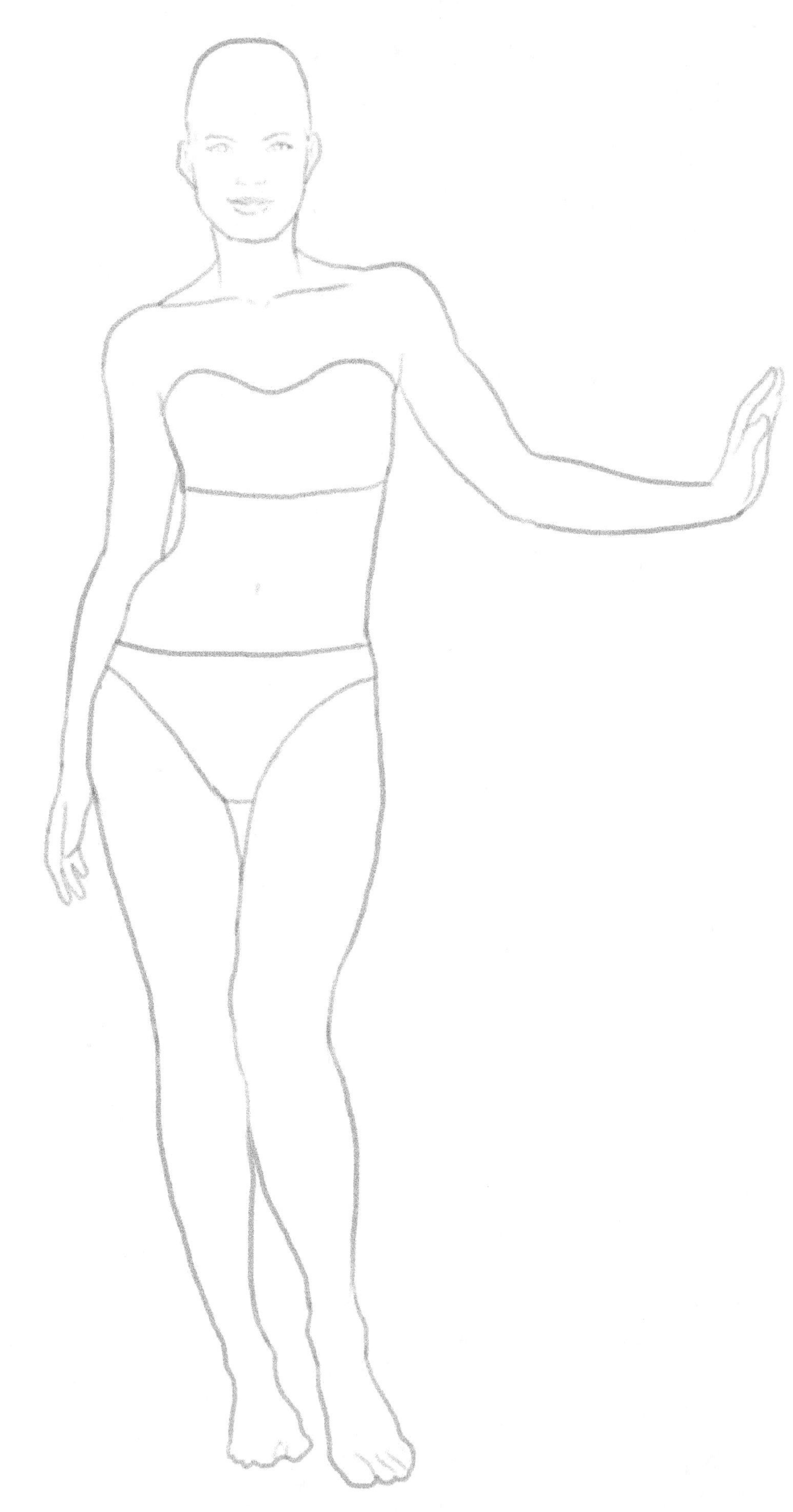

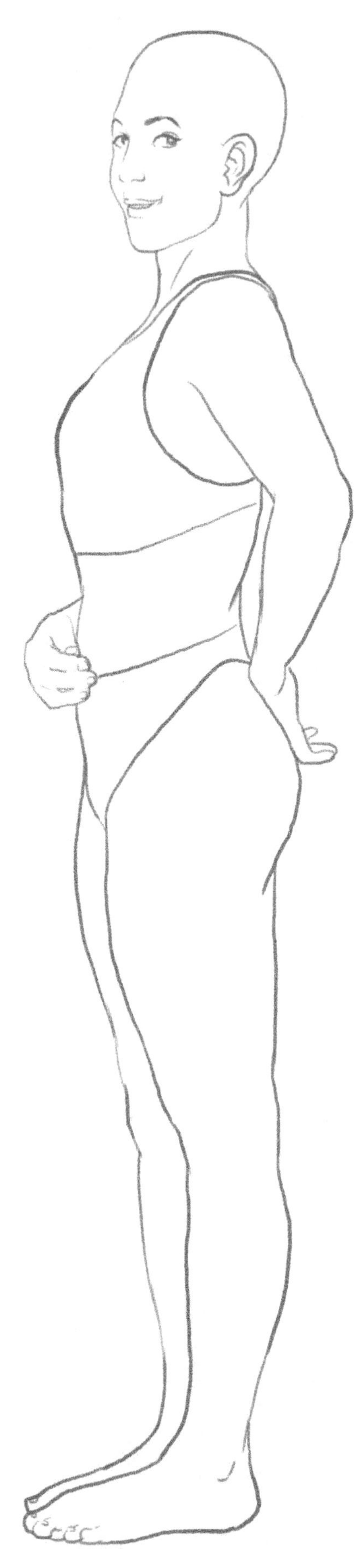

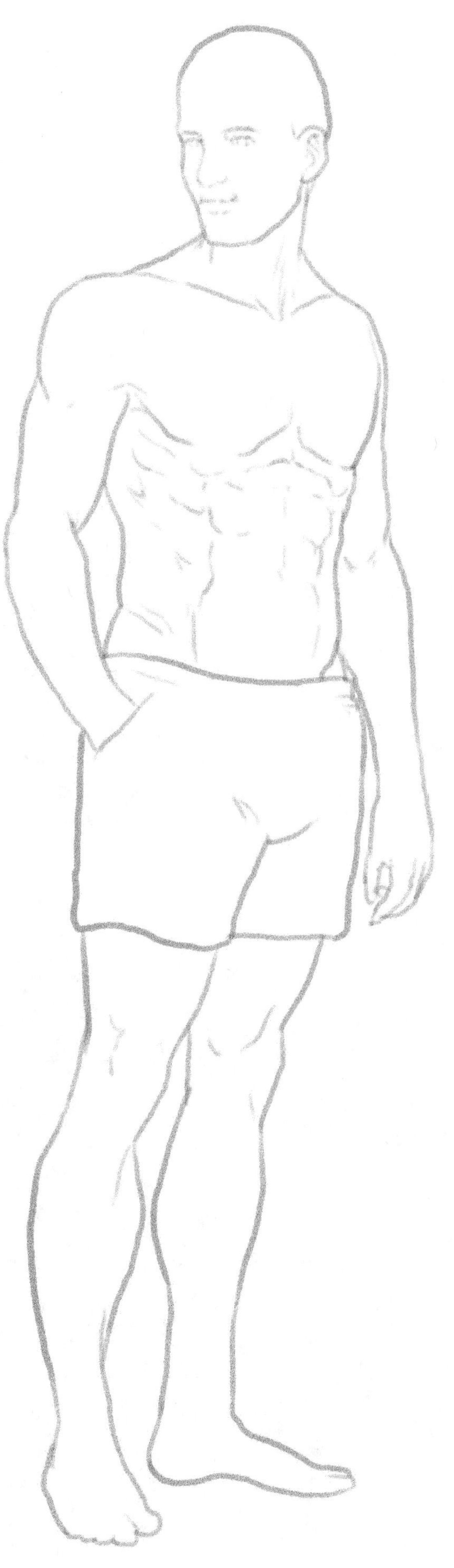

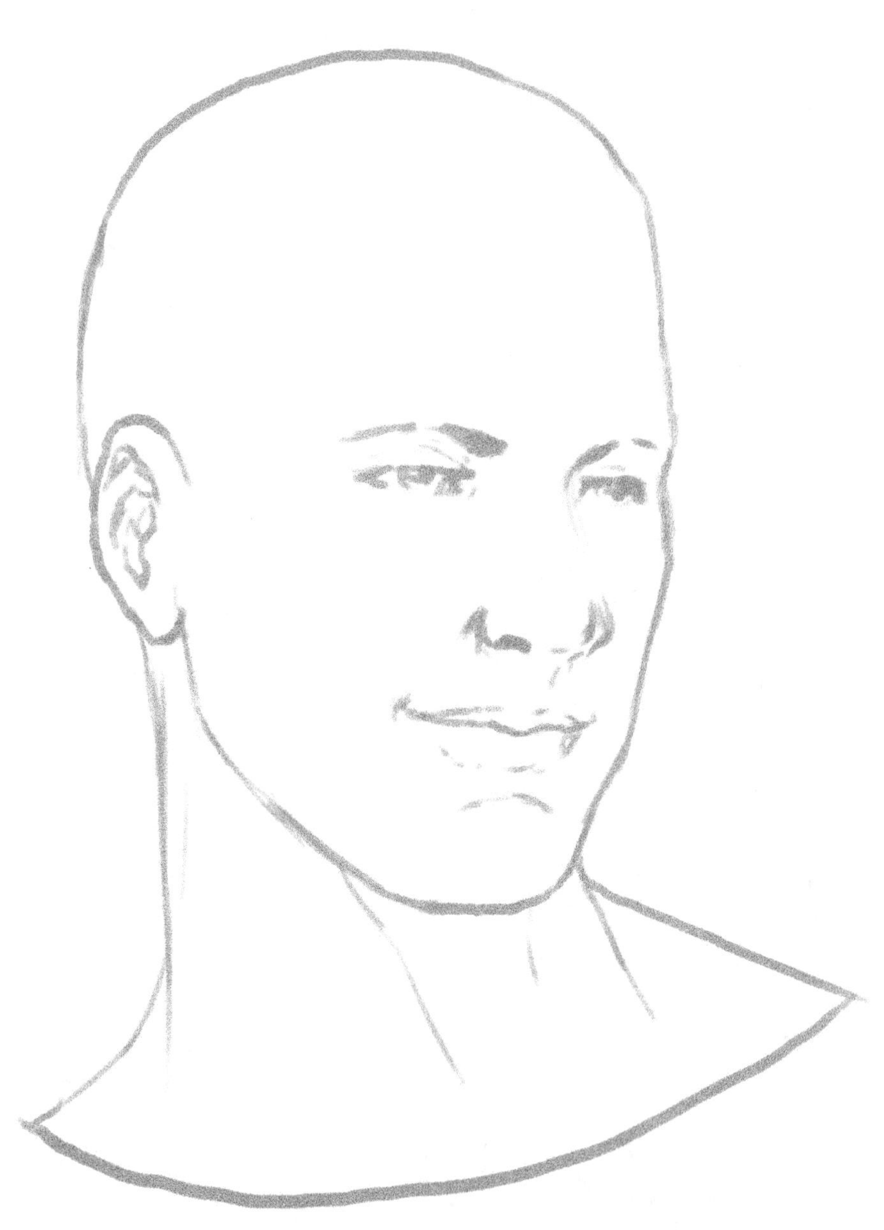

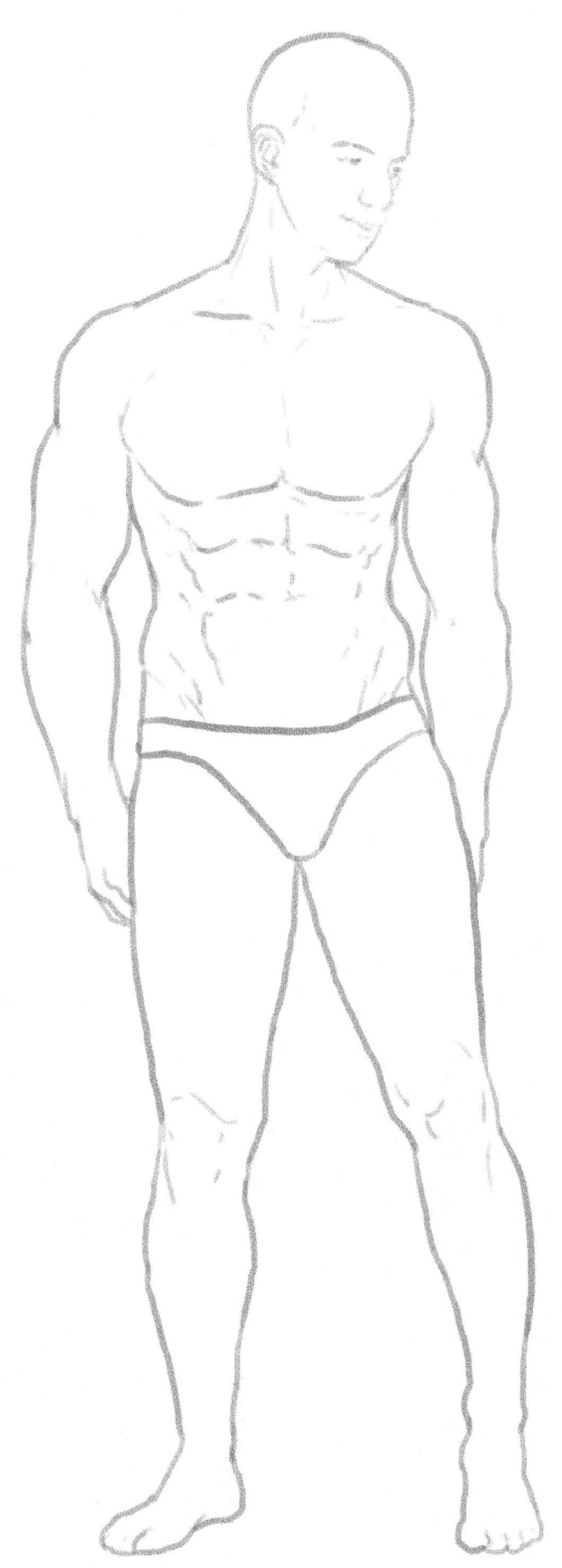

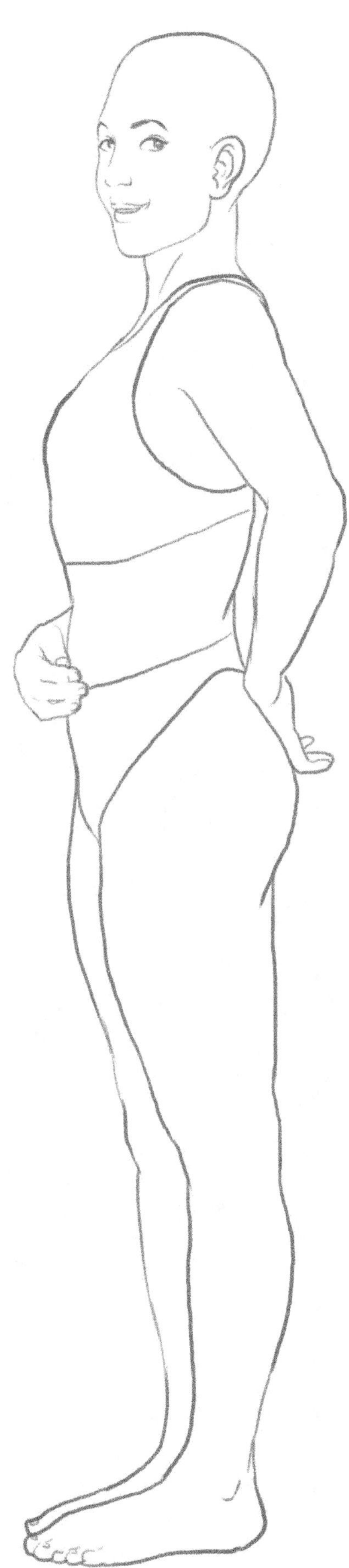

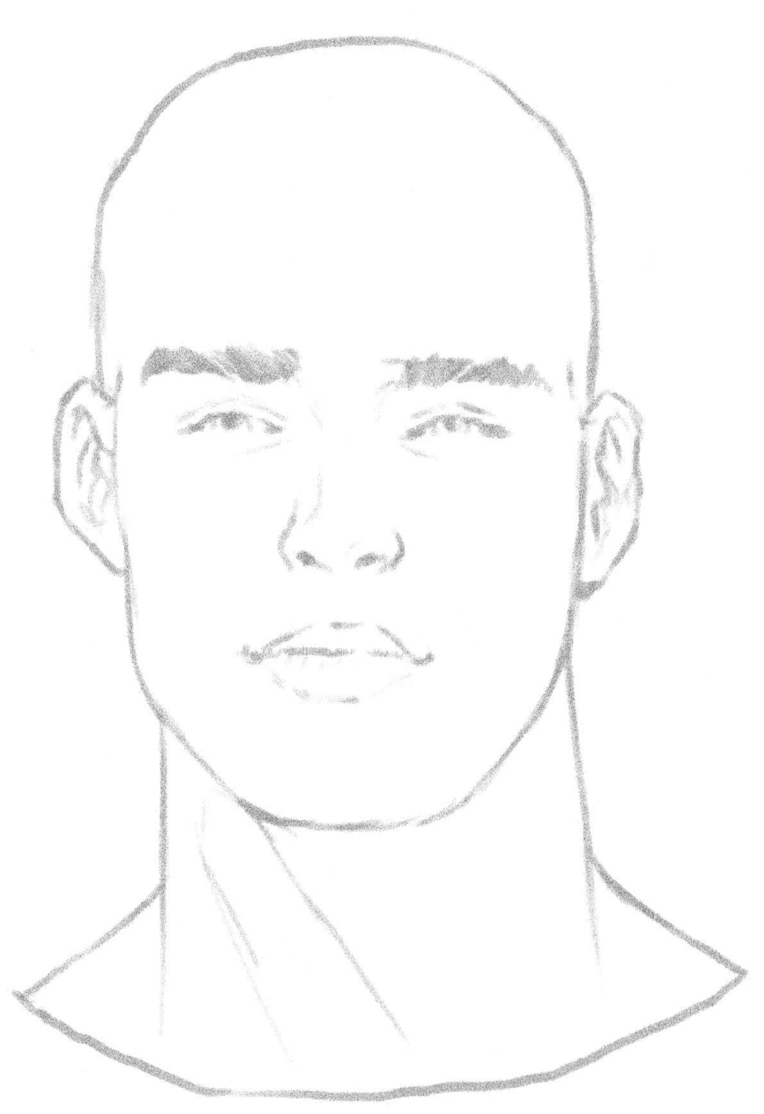

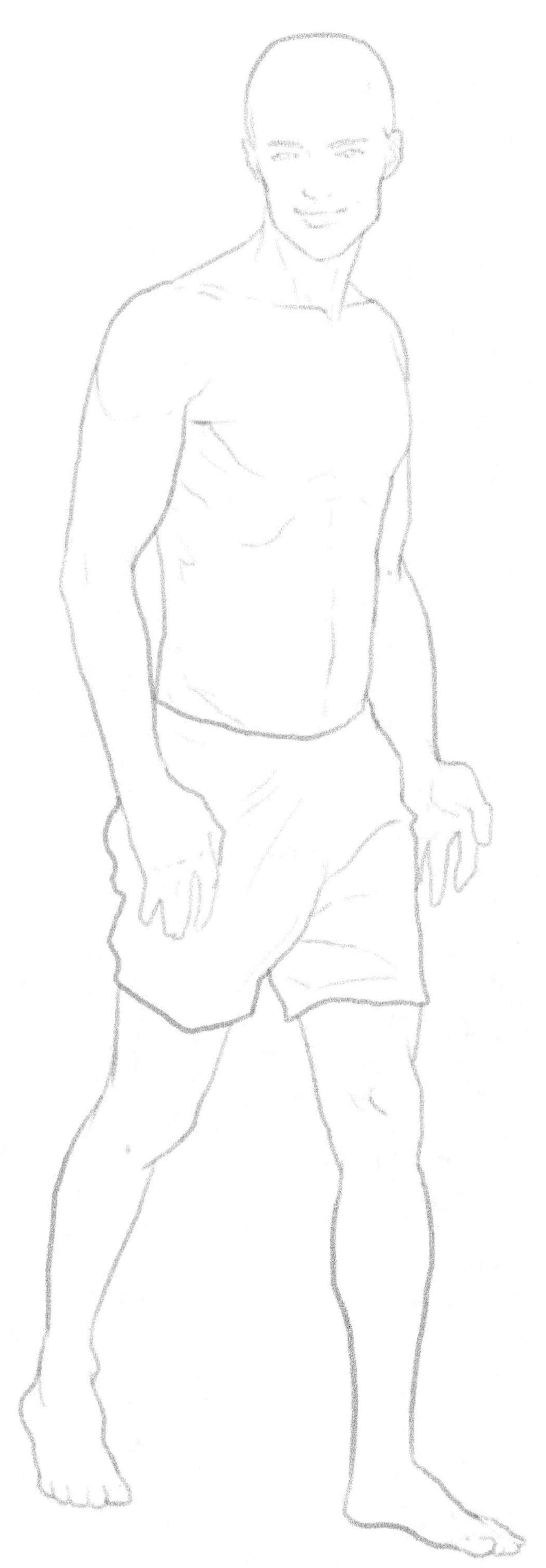

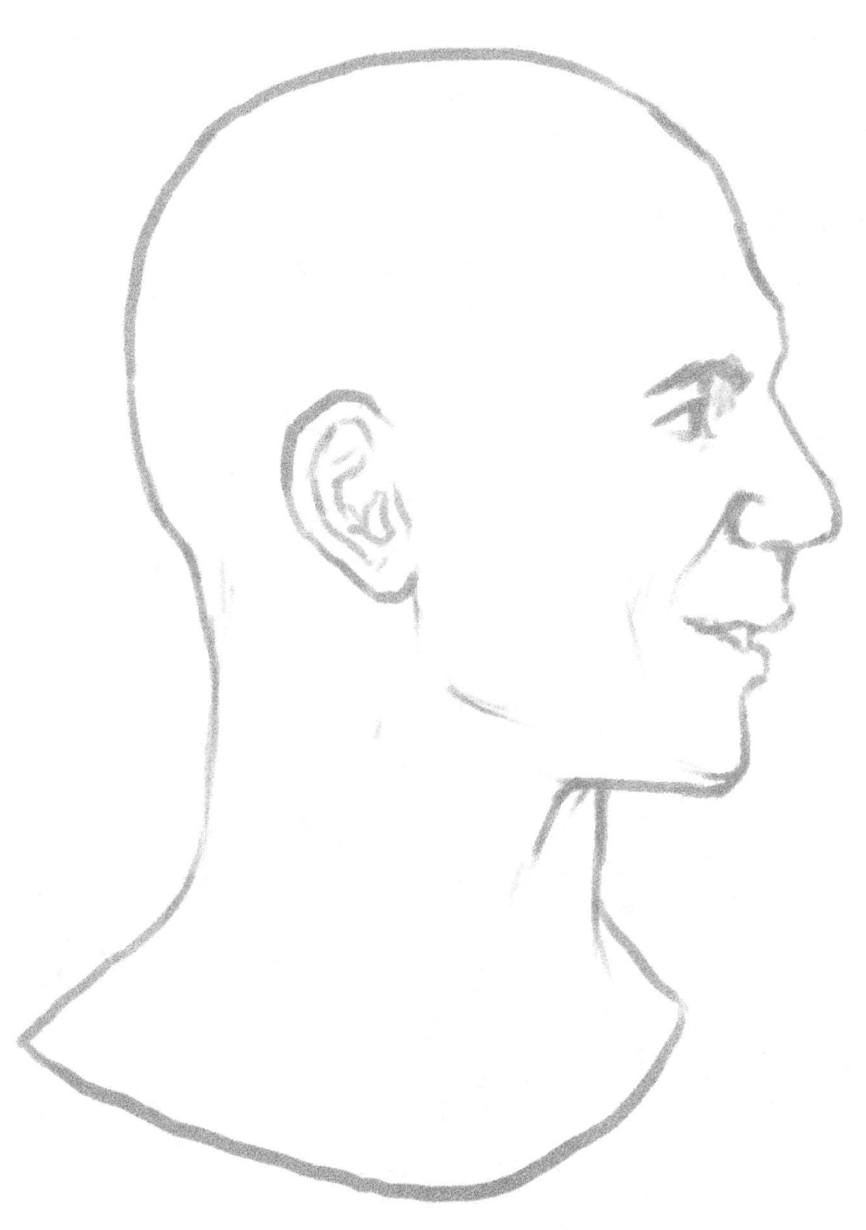

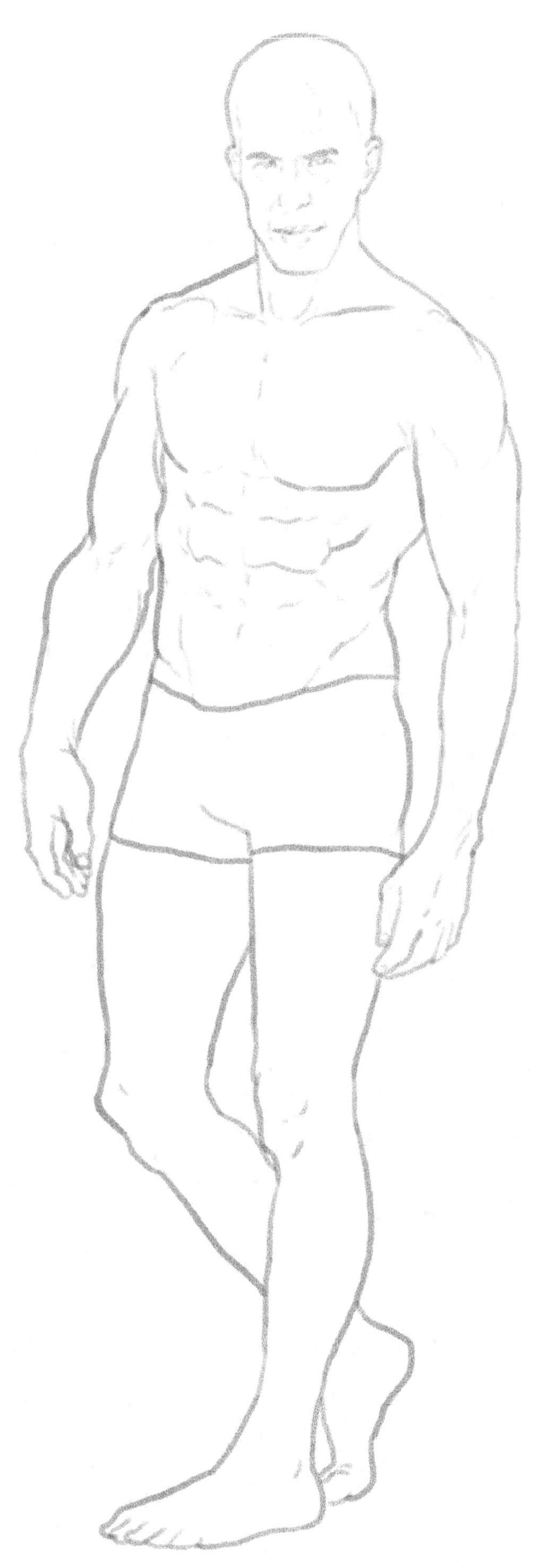

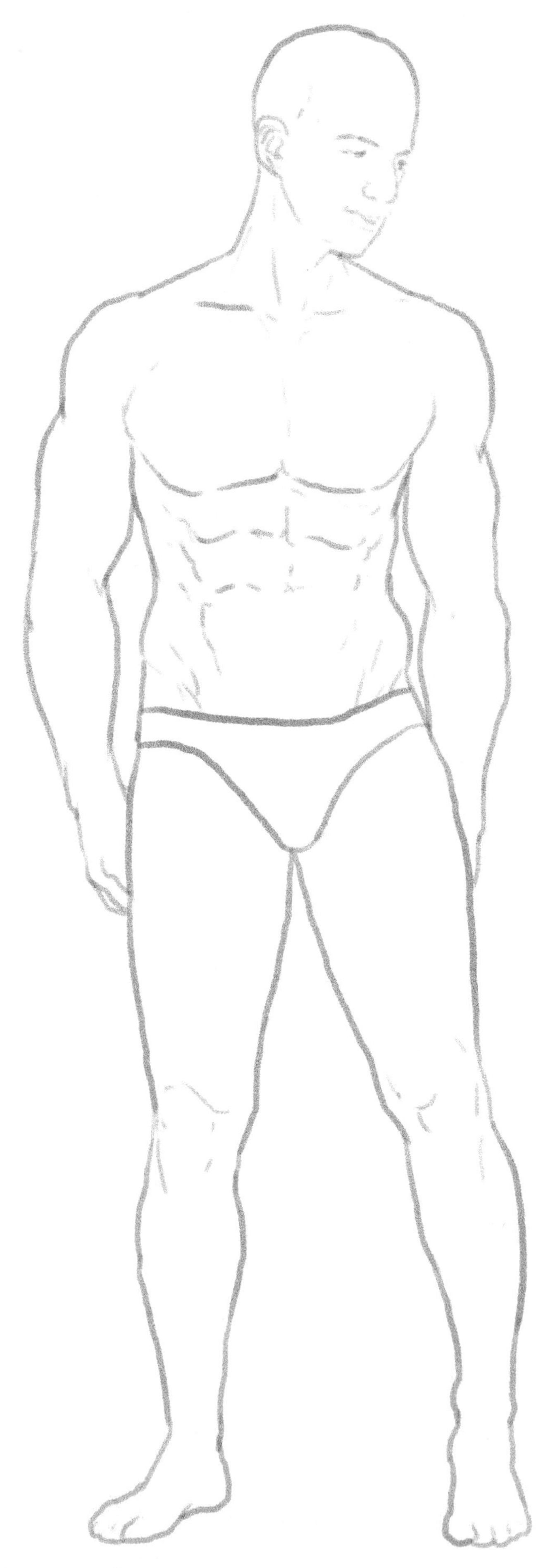

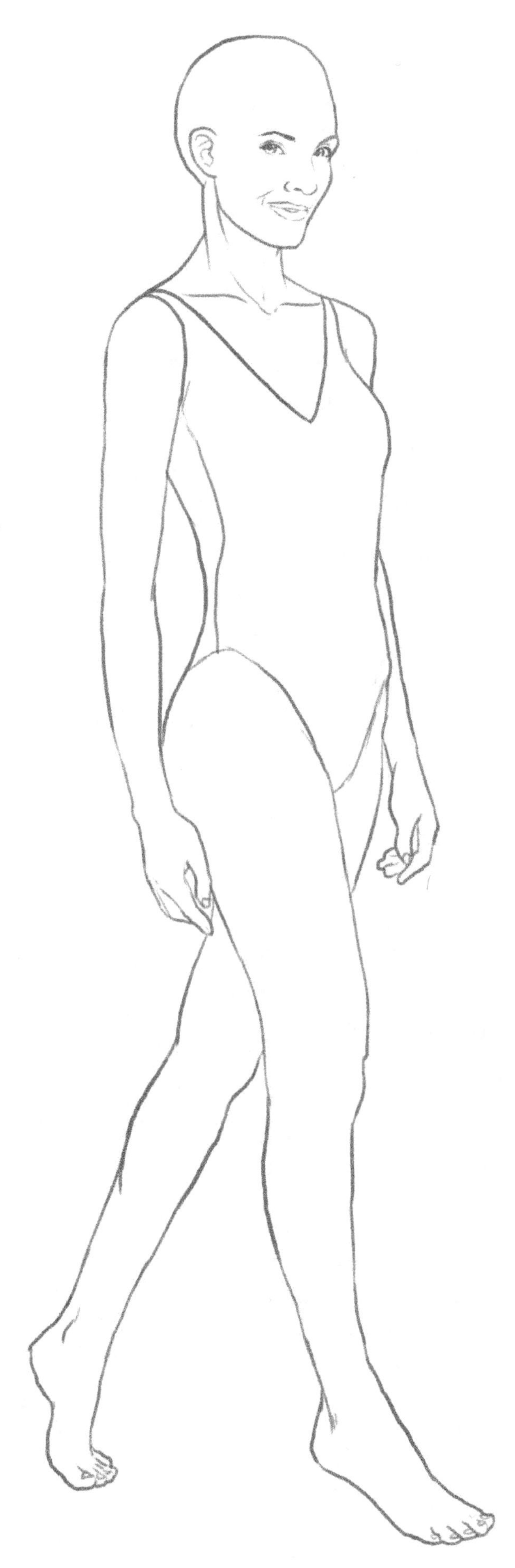

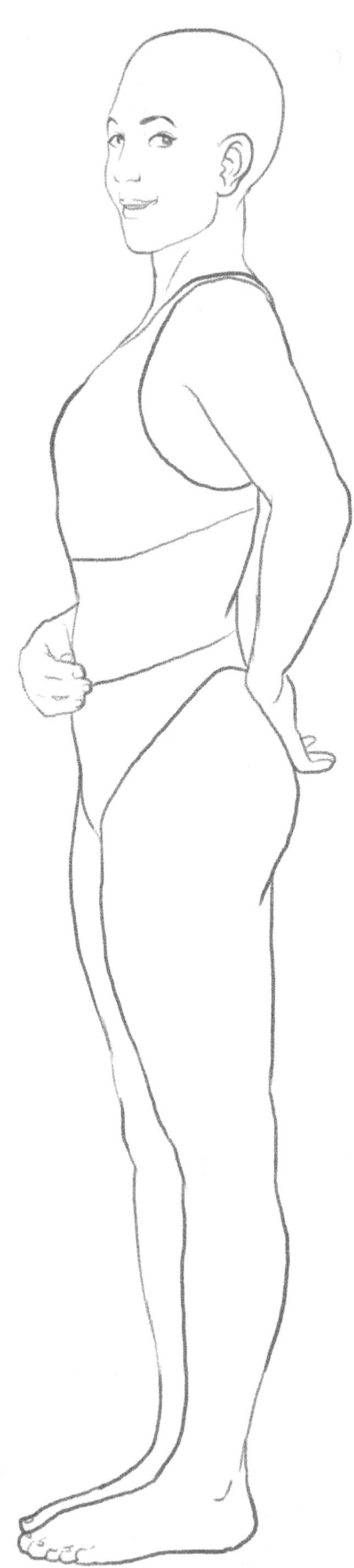

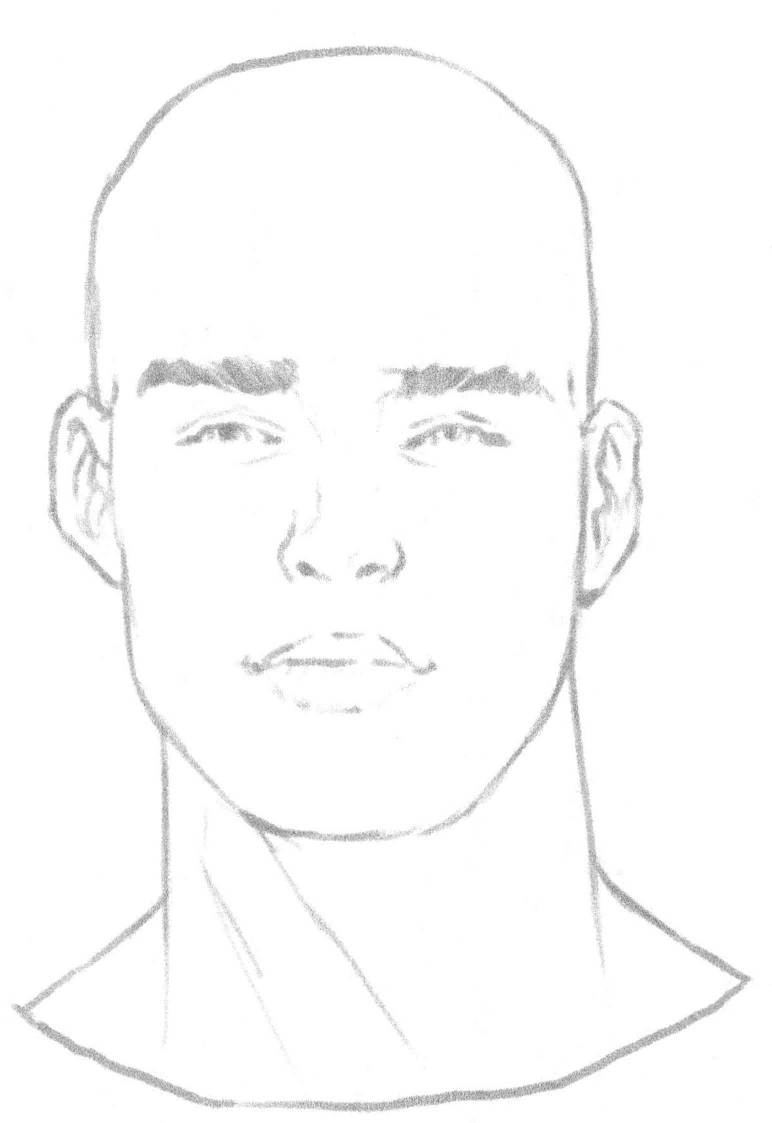

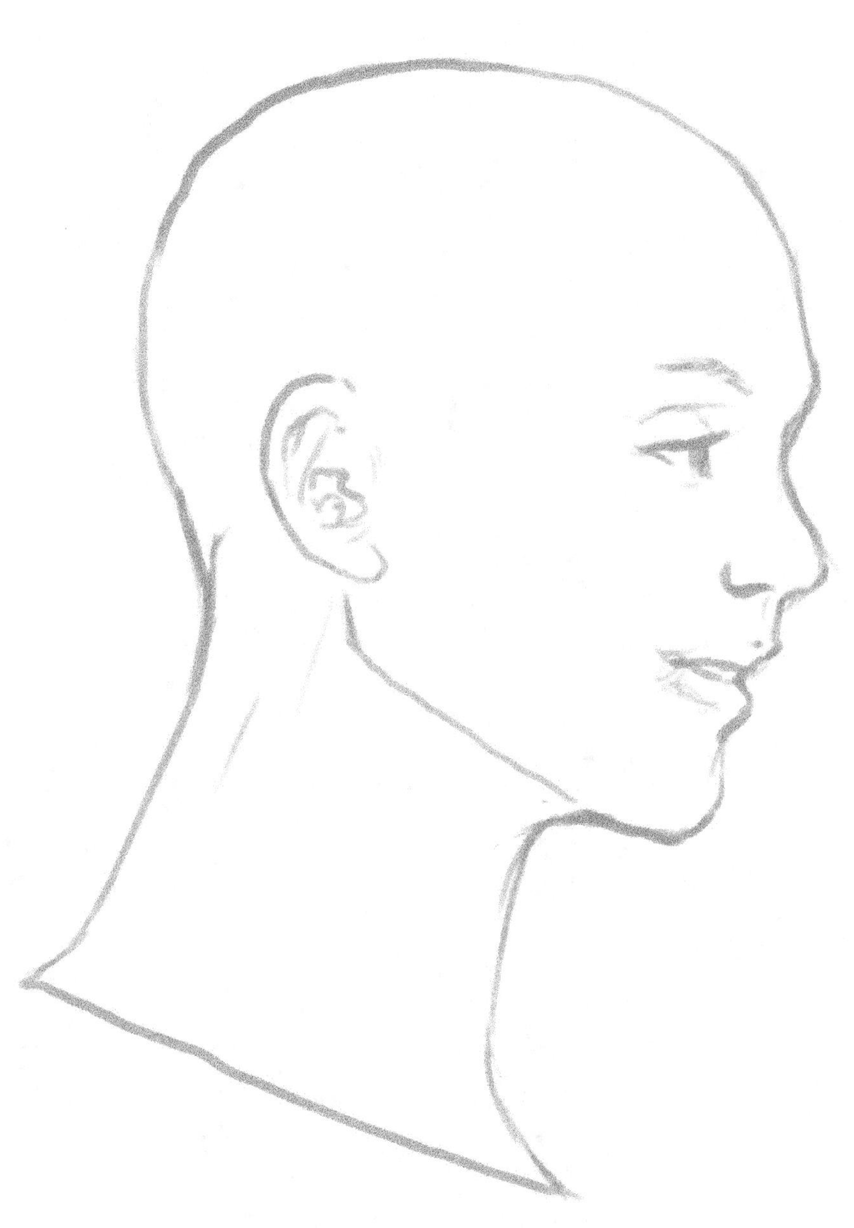

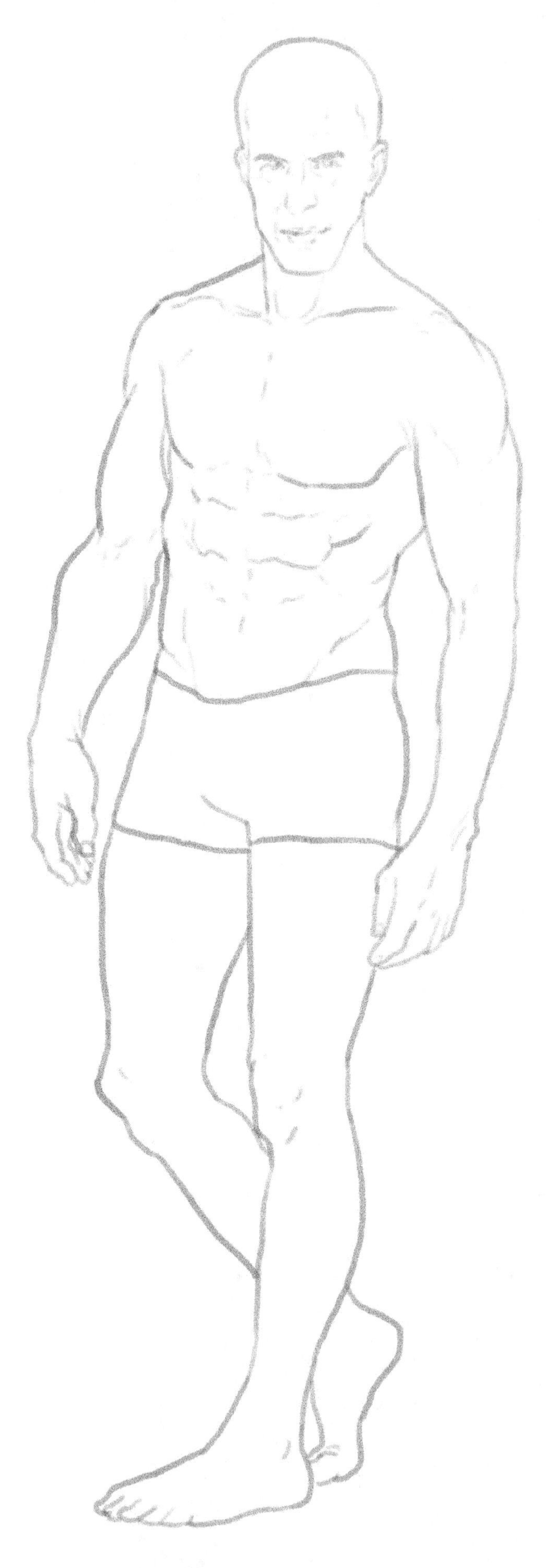

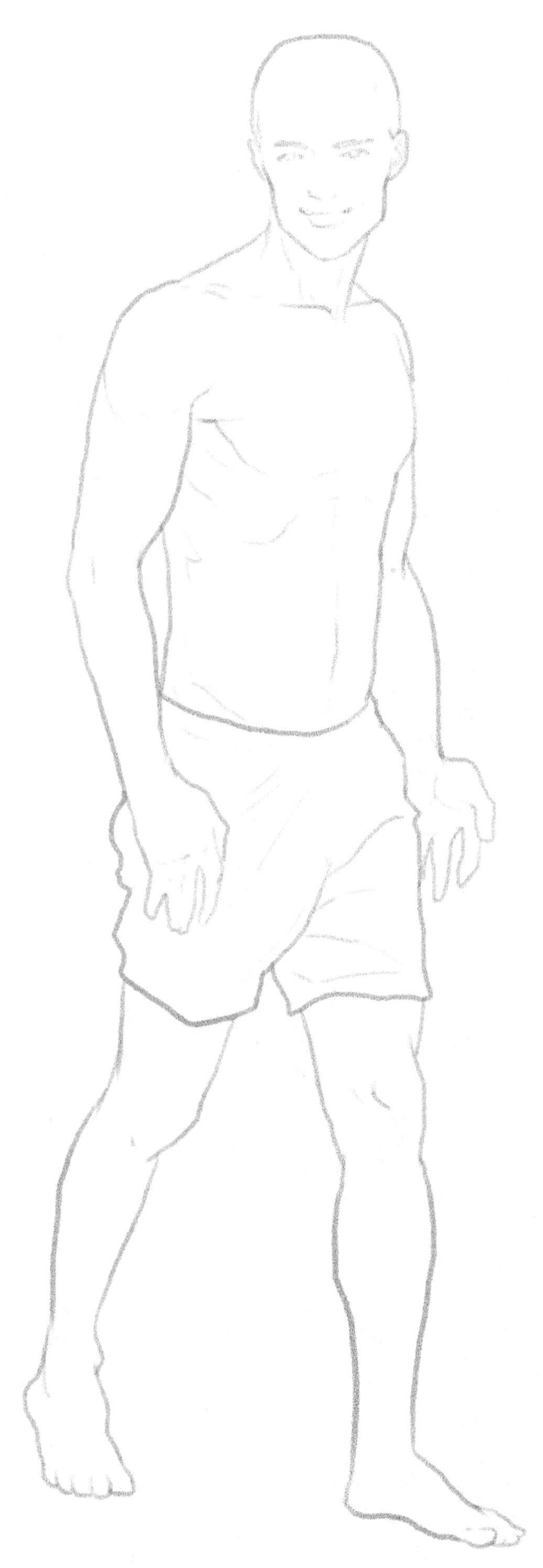

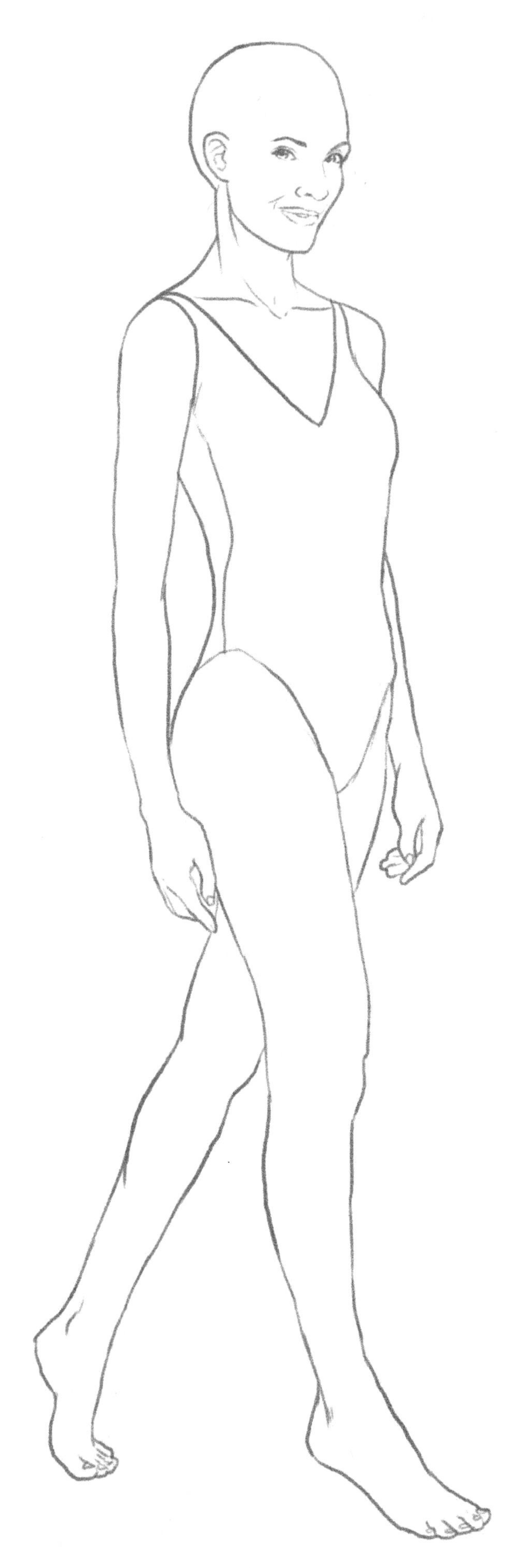

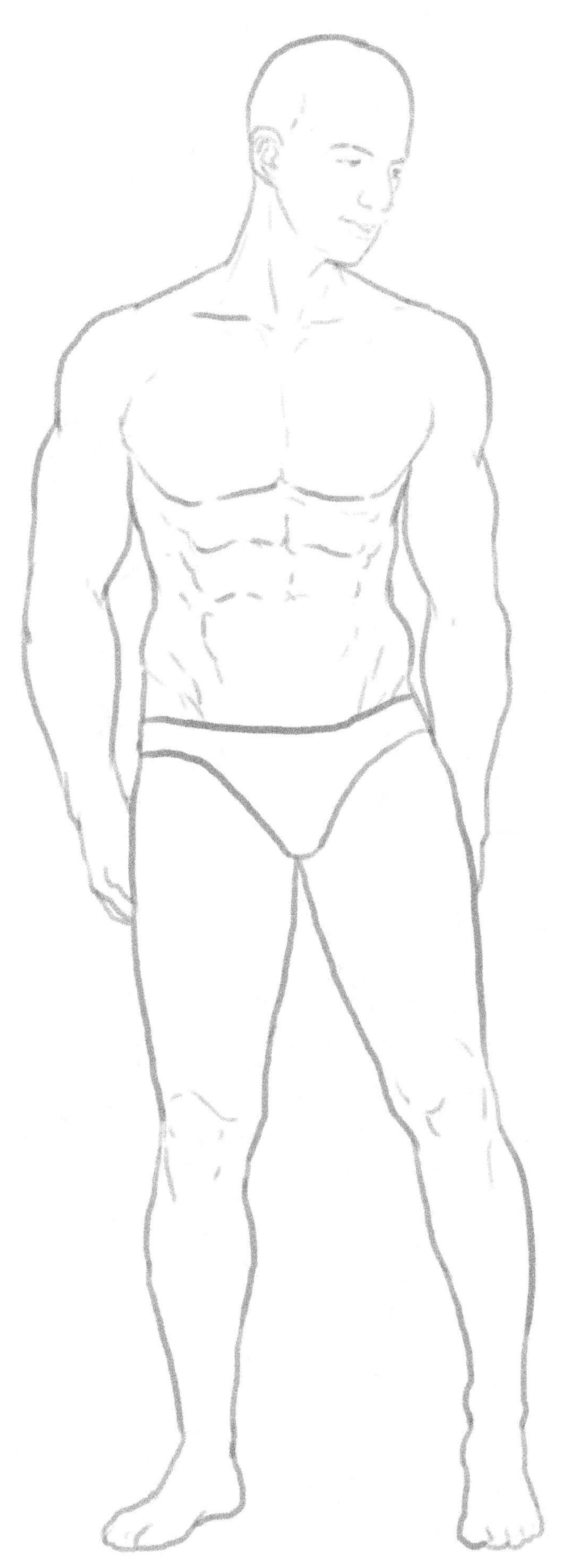

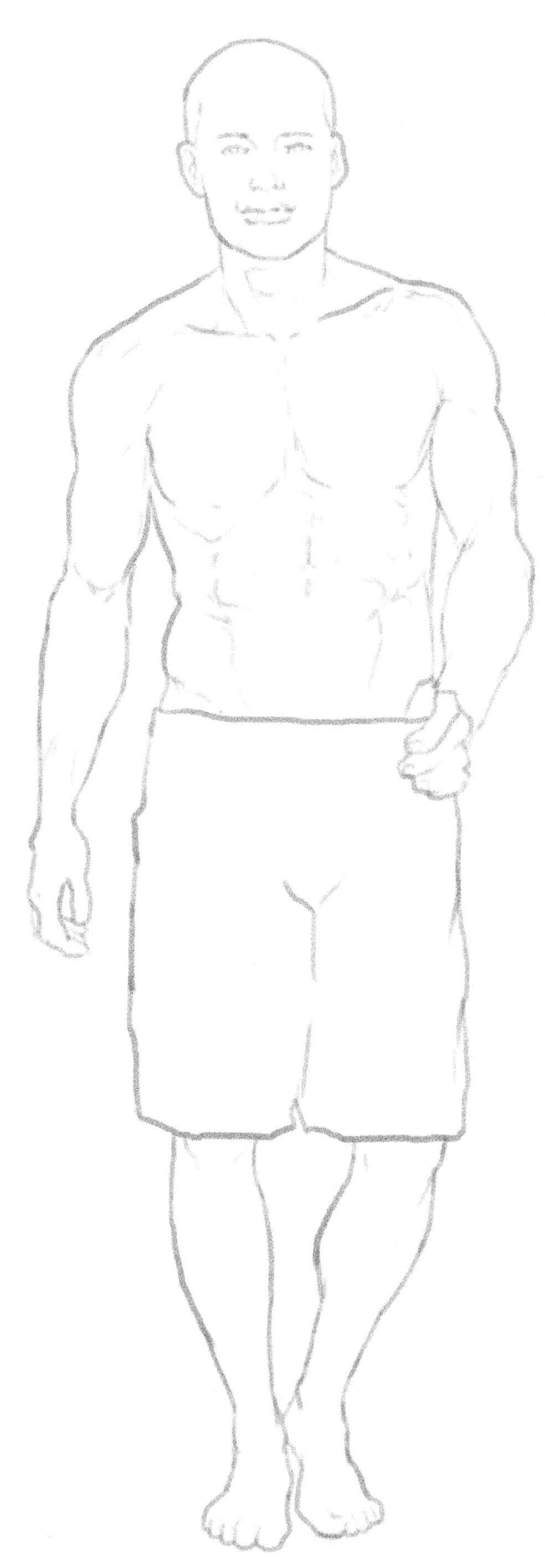

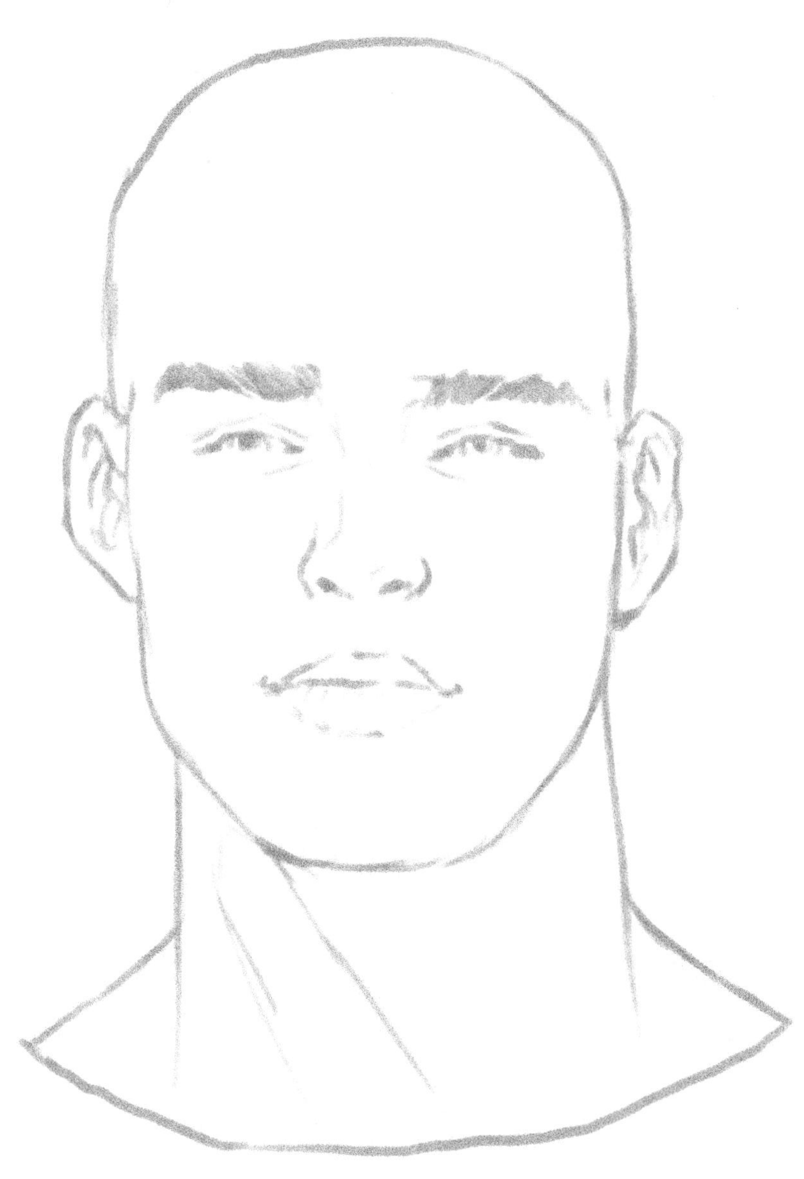

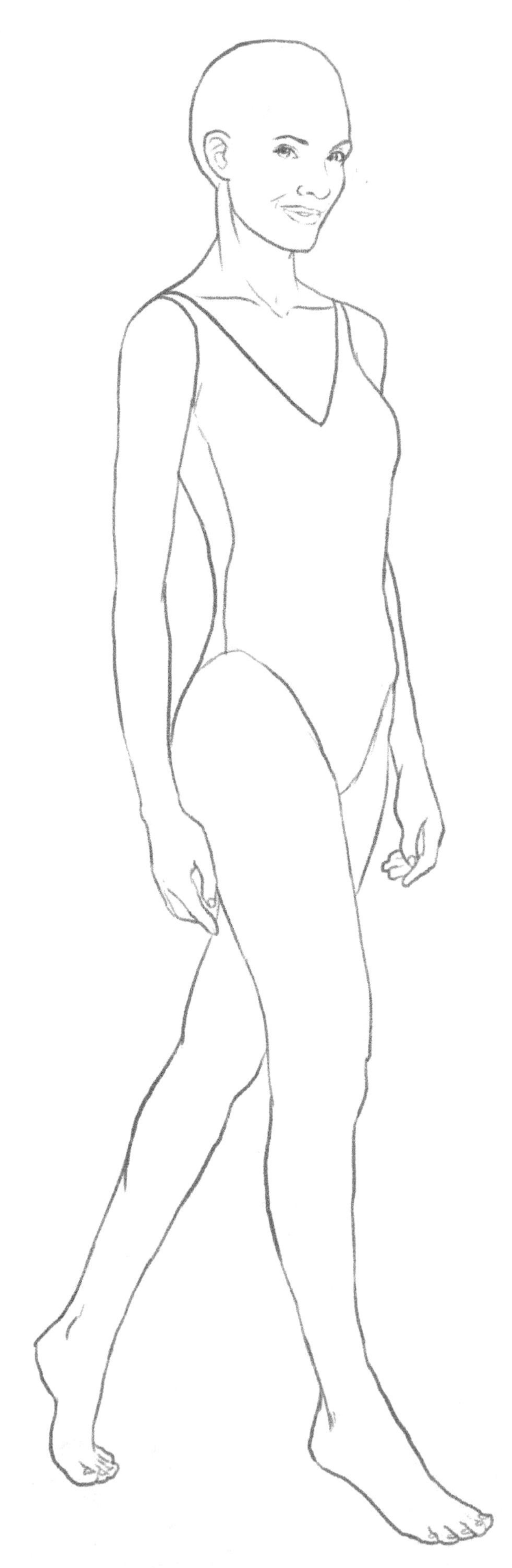

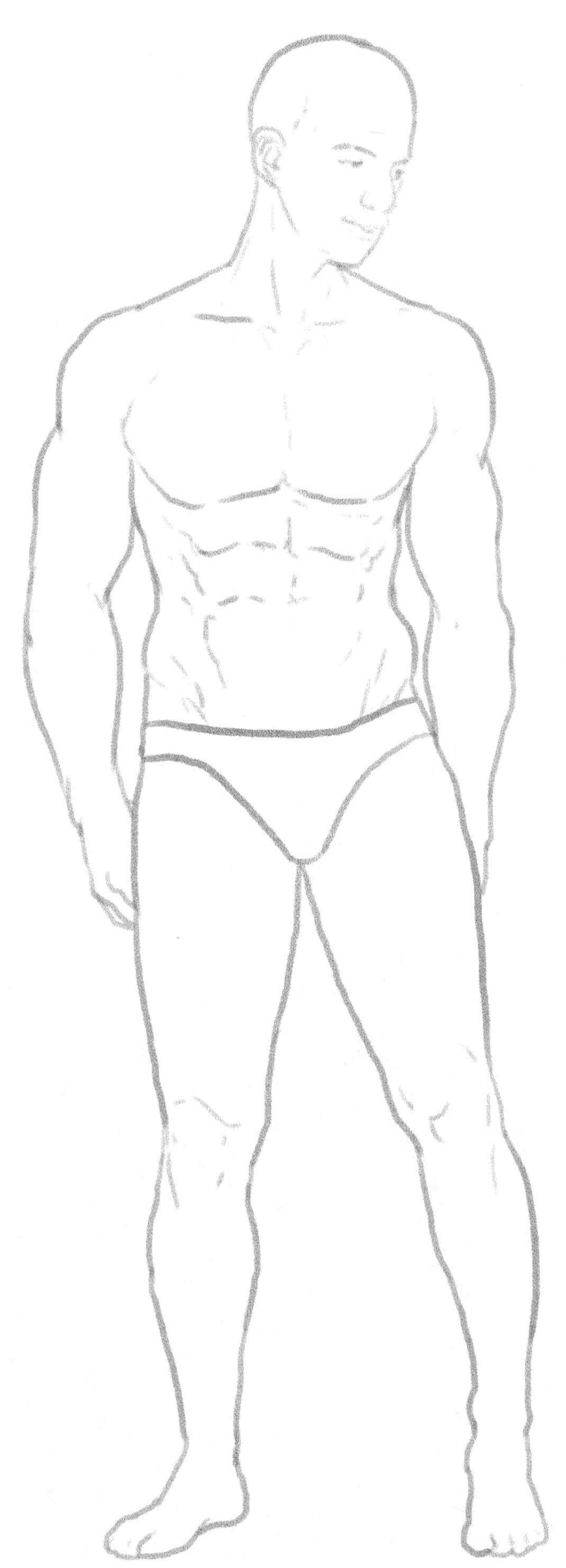

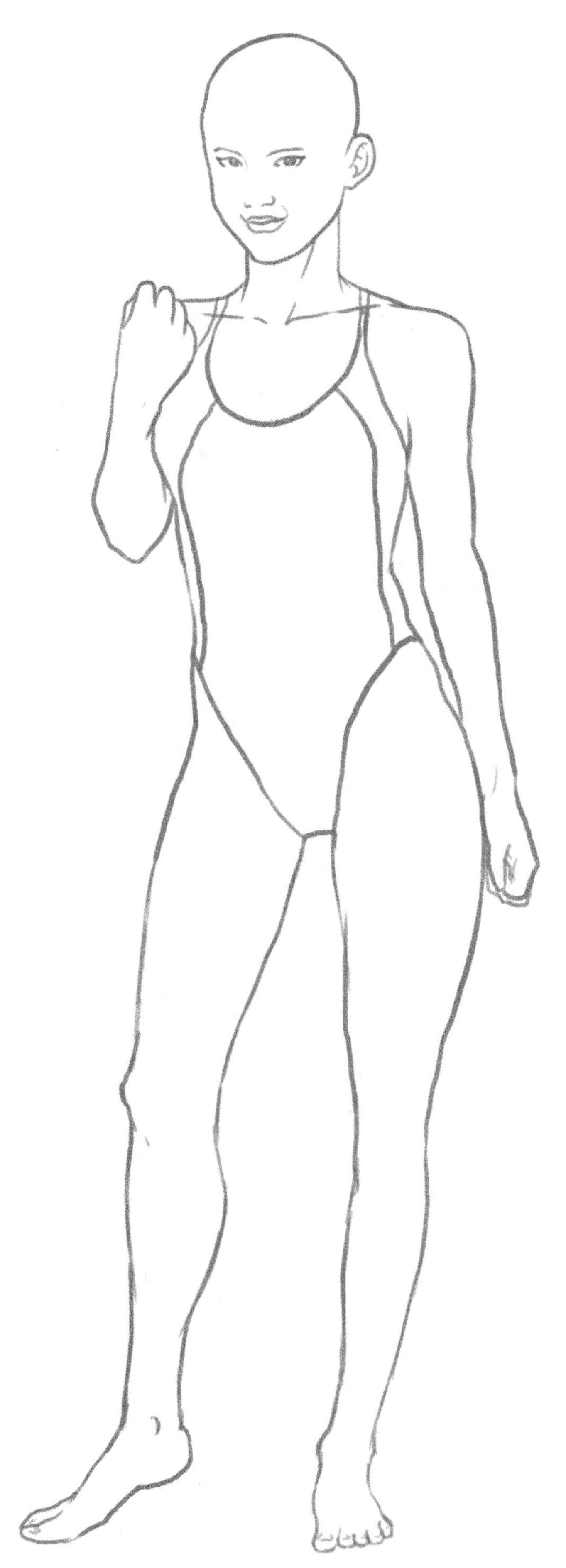

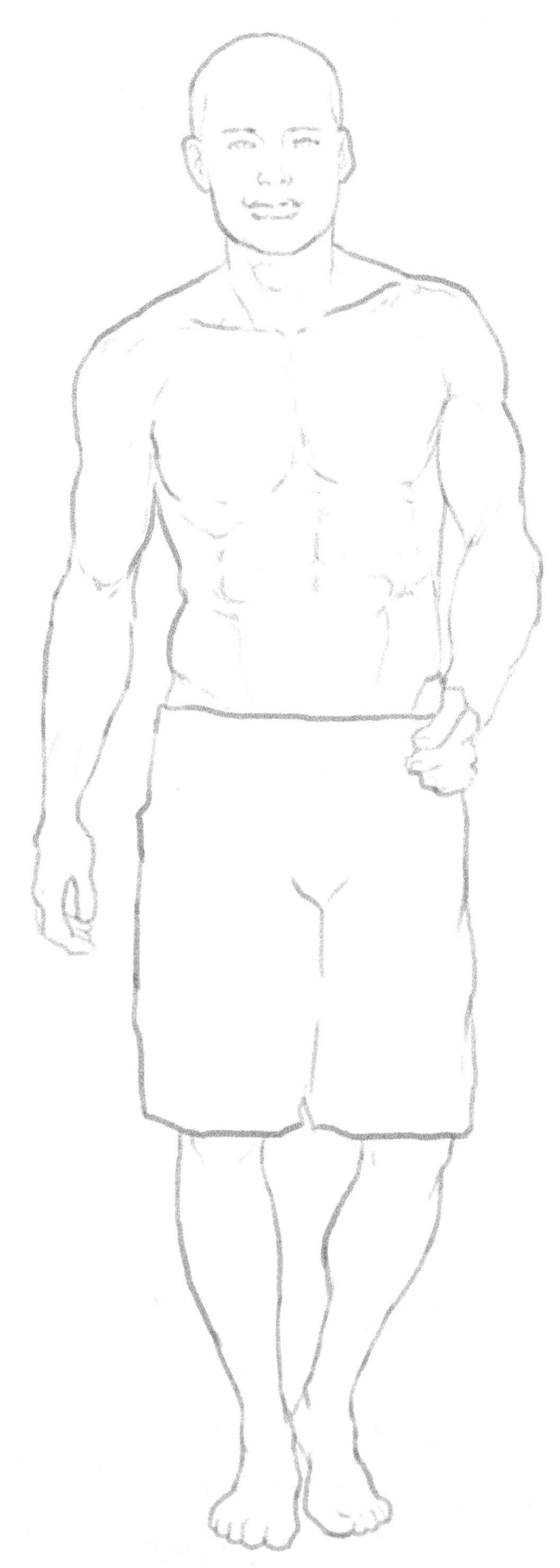

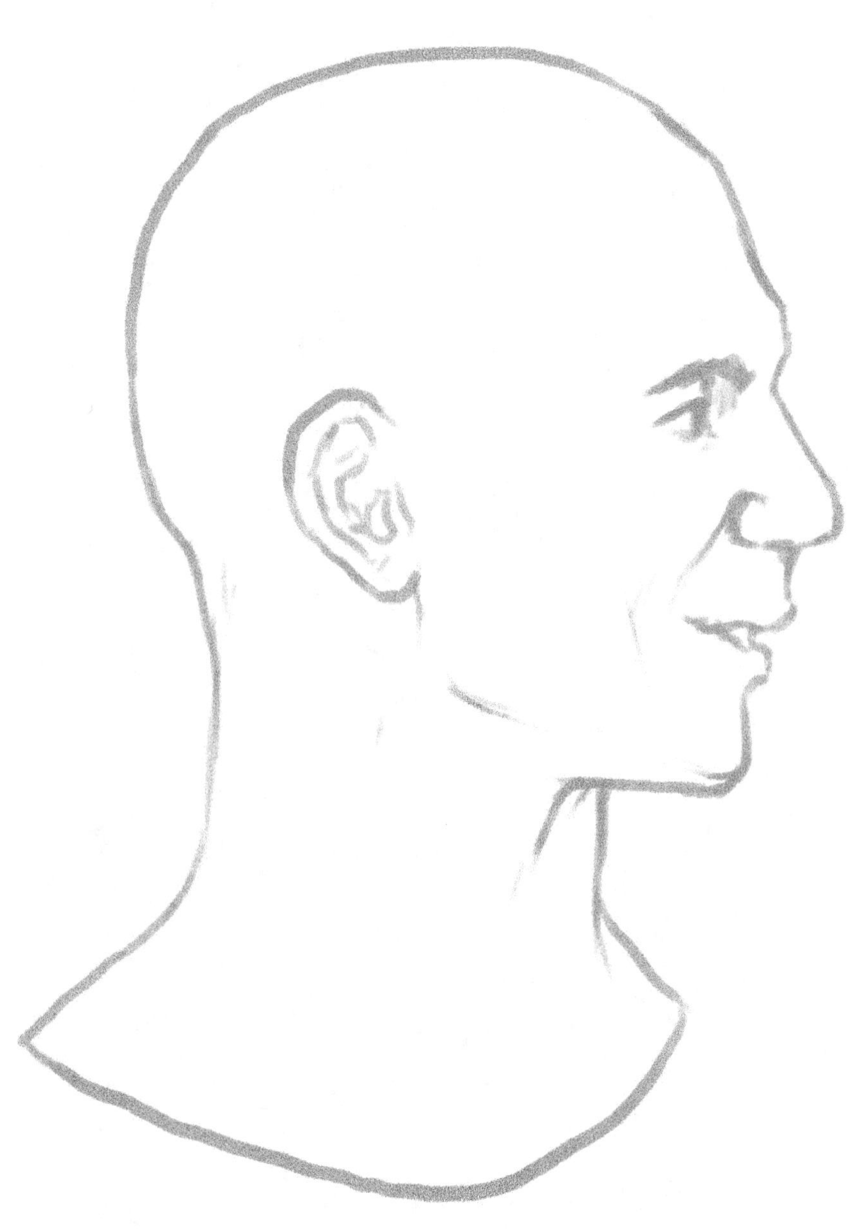